ELECTION SPECIAL — Honolulu Star-Bulletin — IT'S BEN AND MAZIE

Honolulu Star-Bulletin — CLINTON ACQUITTED

Honolulu Star-Bulletin — W9-BZC-946

Insight — BROKEN Trust

Honolulu Star-Bulletin — BISHOP ESTATE TRUSTEES OUSTED — Then there were none

Star Bulletin — DON HO 1930-2007 — We'll Remember You

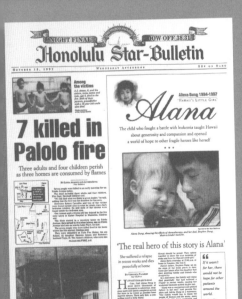

Honolulu Star-Bulletin — 7 killed in Palolo fire — Alana

Honolulu Star-Bulletin — Bush takes over

Star Bulletin — 'THIS RULING IS DISGUSTING'

Star★Bulletin

HONOLULU

HAWAI'I
50

Waikiki. February 19, 1960 (unknown)

Star ★ Bulletin
HONOLULU

HAWAI'I
50
FIVE DECADES
OF PHOTOGRAPHY
A Community Album

Star★Bulletin
HONOLULU

HAWAI'I
50

FIVE DECADES
OF PHOTOGRAPHY

A Community Album

Mutual Publishing

Editors Note

Photographs have been arranged chro-nologi-cally by decade, and within the decade they are dated by when they were taken. In some cases, this date was not available, and the first-run date has been used.

To give readers of *Hawai'i 50* the flavor of the times, captions appear essentially as they did in the *Honolulu Star-Bulletin*, with occasional slight abridgement for space reasons. Usage of Hawaiian language diacriticals—'okina and kahakō—corresponds with the original caption.

Names of people in the photographs are given as they appeared in captions, with occa-sional additions of full names and corrections of spelling. (Very occasionally, correct spelling could not be verified.)

Selection of content was through to July 1, 2008.

Acknowledgements

Special thanks to the following *Star Bulletin* personnel who helped make this book possible: Dennis Francis, President and publisher; Dave Kennedy, vice president marketing; Frank Bridgewater, editor; George Lee, photo editor; Sara Uemura, marketing manager; and Tanya Kogler, executive assistant.

On the Mutual Publishing side, special thanks for their assistance, serving as a sounding board for ideas and helping to bring this project to completion: Gavan Daws, Franco Salmoiraghi, Jane Gillespie, Matthew Martin, Pamela Simon, David Joiner, Erika Roberts, Dawn Sueoka, Courtney Young, Karen Lofstrom, and a big Ma-halo to Gay Wong for all her effort.

Previous Page: Amanda Puamohala Weinstein during the kahiko portion of the Miss Aloha Hula competition at the Merrie Monarch Festival. She belongs to Na Hula O Kaohikukapulani under the direction of kumu hula Kapu Kinimaka-Alquiza. April 12, 2007. (Dennis Oda)

Hawaii 50: Five Decades of Photography, A Community Album
© 2008 Mutual Publishing, LLC

ISBN-10: 1-56647-885-5
ISBN-13: 978-1-56647-885-4

Design/Production by Gonzalez Design

First Printing, October 2008

Mutual Publishing, LLC
1215 Center Street, Suite 210
Honolulu, Hawaii 96816
Ph: (808) 732-1709
Fax: (808) 734-4094
Email: info@mutualpublishing.com
www.mutualpublishing.com

Printed in Korea

CONTENTS

KAMEHAMEH

FOREWORD

Every family has a shoebox stuffed with old family photos—perhaps several boxes, stored in closets, attics, basements and under beds. When later generations dig them up, all too often they will find unmarked photos featuring unidentified people.

Since Hawai'i became a state on August 21, 1959, *Honolulu Star-Bulletin* photographers have shot more than a quarter of a million photographs. We are fortunate that we have not had to cram them into shoeboxes. Old photos have been digitized and, beginning in the early 1990s, we began doing away with our traditional darkroom where we developed film and started using digital cameras. Because a newspaper thrives on facts, our photographers have been good about including names, places and dates when they submitted pictures.

To help commemorate Hawai'i's 50th year of statehood, we have combed through our "shoeboxes" to come up with about 750 of our best and most representative photos, arranged by decades.

If every picture is worth a thousand words, you will find the equivalent of nearly 750,000 words on the following pages. But words, no matter how eloquent, cannot be as breathtaking as pictures, nor can they convey the passion or evoke the feelings of the photos assembled here.

For an individual, 50 years can be a long stretch, even if it may not seem that way when you meet that mark and reflect on the triumphs, tragedies and accomplishments that make up a life.

For a place, a half-century brings with it changes on a much larger scale; there are the traumas of war, political or social revolutions, and the unexpected shocks emanating from nature, economic development and technology. Or the history of a place can be marked by years of relative peace and ease. Or both.

In Hawai'i, five decades of external and homegrown forces have produced changes in myriad ways—though none cataclysmic.

Analysts and historians reviewing the past 50 years will have numerous economic, social and political aspects to dissect, beginning with the first: Statehood, an act that for good or ill, still reverberates through the decades and tinges every moment that was born from it. The Hawaiian Renaissance and Sovereignty movements, the great swell in population in the islands, the quick rise of tourism to become the state's number one industry, the growth of the labor movement and the strikes that followed, and the continued erosion of rural life in the face of unceasing construction, as well as more positive aspects of local life such as the reemergence of pidgin, the rise of local literature, and the blossoming of hula competitions—all derive from that seminal moment.

But this is not a history book—we will leave it to the scholars to chronicle and pass judgment on the past 50 years. This is a community photo album, with nostalgia as the backdrop. The hundreds of photos gathered here reveal our world, emphasizing for the most part those universal ideals, traditions, and triumphs that knit us together, rather than separate us.

So, what do our photos tell us?

We are fascinated by our politicians—maybe because they have always been such a big part of island life and maybe because they're always so entertaining and well-dressed. The decades march along, styles change—suits and oversized campaign buttons give way to heaping piles of lei and aloha shirts tucked in to conservative slacks—politics change, but those smiles, those gleaming, promising, ambitious grins, those have remained the same.

We love our entertainers, too, and the environment that surrounds them. We're always up for live performances and concerts, whether it is inside a Waikīkī hotspot or outside in Diamond Head Crater or the Waikiki Shell. And they don't have to be big events; we just love to be entertained—any performer in any venue will do.

Looking at how often they appeared in the paper, and the size of their funerals, we worshipped Don Ho, Braddah Iz, Rell Sunn, and Gabby—all Hawaiians it should be noted. In so many ways, they were Hawai'i, and the unique, loving forces of aloha they generated continue to bathe the Earth.

We are enamored of pageants and competitions of all sorts. It would be a safe bet to assume that Hawai'i is the only place in the world where one can find beauty pageants representing nearly every ethnicity in the Pacific Rim. If it isn't beauty pageants we're craving, it's hula. The Merrie Monarch festival, with its pomp, circumstance and just a bit of Las Vegas showiness thrown in, holds us in thrall every spring as we watch halau take the stage of the Hilo Civic Center.

The keiki of Hawai'i are the cutest kids in the world. We delight in their antics and playfulness. They turn simple, everyday moments of life into pure joy, for themselves and for all of us watching.

Throughout the years, our kūpuna have been front and center. They show up regularly in the paper, obviously cherished by families and friends. They hold a magical place in the hearts of everyone, preserving culture and the gentle Hawaiian way of life, passing it on to the next generation.

Not surprisingly, a lot of our photos involve outdoor activities. We are always outside fishing, surfing, hiking, paddling, running, bicycling, picnicking and just hanging out with family.

Whenever a new store opens, we are all over it. And whenever landmarks are demolished, we mourn—but we do not forget them, indeed, we continue to refer to them long after they're gone.

Above: This father and his three children take a "scenic" tour of the Ala Wai Canal, dodging debris, of course. The Ala Wai seems dirtier than usual this week after heavy rains. January 19, 1975. (Warren R. Roll)

Sometimes we protest. We mass at the state capitol for physical shows of opposition. We listen to impassioned speakers. We march. We wave signs. What pushes us to the point of protest? It might be a belief that sacred land is under attack or that some group is not being treated fairly.

Mother Nature never lets us forget who is in charge, constantly interrupting our lives with storms, hurricanes and threats of hurricanes, and torrential downpours that occasionally lead to flooding. There are also less frequent but sometimes scary and too often destructive earthquakes and volcanic eruptions. When we are very lucky, these events only amount to a loss of property, some mud inside the house, an increase in insurance deductibles, and some frayed nerves. When we are not so lucky, all feel the loss.

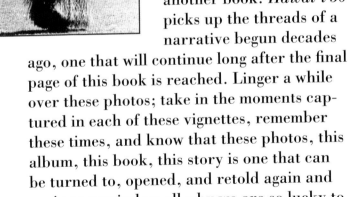

The common thread that runs throughout is the enduring beauty of our islands—the sunsets, landscapes, visions of clouds scudding across the tops of peaks, the absolute, arresting green of a valley, shadows cradled deep within the folds of mountains, sunlight beating down on beaches. We cling to these scenes that touch some sentimental parts of ourselves and form part of a collective past that increasingly eludes us.

We were not sure what to expect when we started sifting through our shoeboxes. We thought that perhaps photos of breaking news would dominate—crimes and accidents, in particular—but what prevailed was an abundance of good times and blissful everyday scenes that are often taken for granted. Knowing that family photo albums concentrate on the positive, we decided to play down the unpleasant except in a few cases where those photos were so dramatic.

The *Star-Bulletin* felt strongly about wanting to commemorate the golden anniversary of Hawai'i's statehood in a way that only we could. We realize that a minority regret statehood for various reasons, including the loss of culture and older ways of living. From a geopolitical point of view, Hawai'i had little chance of escaping the priorities and rivalries of the world superpowers. But those are issues for another book. *Hawai'i 50* picks up the threads of a narrative begun decades ago, one that will continue long after the final page of this book is reached. Linger a while over these photos; take in the moments captured in each of these vignettes, remember these times, and know that these photos, this album, this book, this story is one that can be turned to, opened, and retold again and again to remind us all why we are so lucky to live Hawai'i.

Frank Bridgewater
Editor
Honolulu Star-Bulletin

Above: Tourists Delight-The Kodak Hula Show. May 3, 1966. (Albert Yamauchi)

PREFACE

The *Honolulu Star-Bulletin* is honored to share with you *Hawai'i 50: Five Decades of Photography A Community Album*—a compilation of some of our best photographs of the last fifty years, full of compelling images of this astounding place we call home.

To select and present these photos in the best way possible, we have teamed up with Mutual Publishing, one of Hawai'i's largest book publishers. Mutual has extensive experience in producing picture histories and illustrated books, which we think has blended well with our strength in chronicling Hawai'i's history.

Together, we have reviewed about a quarter-million *Star-Bulletin* photos taken since Hawai'i became a state on Aug. 21, 1959. That means the photos in this book represent a mere 0.003 percent of those we took during those years. They are truly the best of the best.

As reference points, we have reprinted newspaper front pages from various eras, to remind us of events that were important

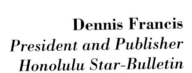

(or perhaps amusing) at the time.

We invited Franco Salmoiraghi, a longtime local photo journalist, to write an introduction sharing his insights on photo journalism, to help put the assemblage of photos in perspective.

We also have included creations from Corky, our incomparable cartoonist, who has been reminding us of the amusing side of Island life for the past forty years.

Our reasons for publishing this community photo album are twofold. First, we were so mesmerized by the photos that we believed we had to share them. Second, by publishing this book, we will help make Hawai'i an even better place, because we are donating some proceeds from the sale of the book to benefit local charities supported by the *Star-Bulletin*. We are proud to continue a 126-year history of civic participation and involvement.

Dennis Francis
President and Publisher
Honolulu Star-Bulletin

Opposite page: The Duke Kahanamoku Statue in Waikiki. September 9, 2005. (Dennis Oda)
Above: Elvis performing at the Honolulu Stadium, where the most expensive seat in the house was $3.50. November 10, 1957. (Jack Matsumoto)

INTRODUCTION

Who are these newspaper photographers that seem to descend out of nowhere into the middle of events and situations, buzzing around with their cameras and flash units, the pockets of their safari vests bulging with photo gear and notepads?

For them, every situation in life is a target of opportunity. They appear, photograph you—fifty times in high-speed bursts—from above and below, and then they are gone.

Newspaper photographers are constantly watching and calculating how to get an edge. They move in closer for a clearer look, monitoring the light and the changing situation until, suddenly, something happens and they move to zero in on their target while the clock ticks down to deadline time.

There is excitement, and then there is routine. They work every day on assignment—spot news, sports, community events, features, fillers—whatever the day brings or doesn't bring.

Most days in Honolulu are ordinary—a ball game, a canoe race, the opening of a school, the first day of the legislature, traffic gridlock, maybe a perp walk. Familiar things. The trick—actually, the craft and the skill of the job—is to turn an ordinary happening into something visually out of the ordinary.

On the slowest news days, the photographer's assignment may be to "Go out and find something." This is called "Wild Art"—perhaps something as simple as a sunset with an interesting foreground, someone fishing or playing with their kids, someone sleeping, or a little girl walking a big, big dog. Sometimes nothing happens. But that nothing is often the biggest event happening, so they must be able to photograph nothing. They must make an interesting picture for the editor waiting in the newsroom: a picture that tells a story—even a story about nothing. They must be patient. They must sit and wait, talk with people, and be friendly.

And their photographs must be accurate and truthful in intent, even though not all newspaper photographs are candid. Many are set up, created specifically for the photo op. The truth we think we are seeing is sometimes a fictional narrative passing for reality. But it must be honest fiction and not misrepresent the veracity of the situation or the people portrayed.

Even in mundane circumstances, these photographers are looking for the image that catches a memorable, decisive moment in a way that makes it last. When the newspaper is gone—used to wrap the garbage, or to clean up the oil spill in the garage, or recycled at the neighborhood school–photographers want their pictures to live on in your memory.

In the back of their minds is the possibility, or at least the hope, that an amazing image will appear out of nowhere. Long Vegas odds that this will happen, this gamble of being in exactly the right place at exactly the right moment. But then newspaper photographers are gamblers who keep coming back for more. Looking deeply with their vision and their perceptions attuned to an inner sense of navigation toward the news, they aim for the heart of a story.

They are searching for *the* shot, the one that will jump off the page, catch the eye, and burn into the memory. That is the work of the

The voyaging, double hulled, canoe, *Hokulea* under full sail off Diamond Head. June, 1980. (Ken Sakamoto)

photojournalist—on the street, day after day, anticipating that fleeting crack in time when the universe may conspire to put a Pulitzer Prize-winning moment in front of their camera.

Those instants are brief and very rare, but the job is to remain adroit and proficient, skillful, competent, and masterly while making images that will live on in our collective memory—the photographer's own version of forever. This requires a constitutional capacity to perform day after day, functioning at a high level of physical, mental, and technical complexity. And the photographer must maintain a state of conscious awareness in every situation, abiding by the photojournalists' code of no harsh or unethical practices: No setting up reenactments of spot news and passing them off as the event itself. No digital manipulation of the image. Communicate accurate captions of the event. Be nice to the subjects, bystanders, cops, fire-men, and other photographers.

Photographs could be forever, but most are not. They are fragile—paper, gelatin, acetate, pixels. Some survive, more disappear. They can be destroyed or vanish in an instant. And with them, history and memory. It is amazing that so many survive.

The *Honolulu Star-Bulletin* archive holds more than 250,000 photographs. More than a quarter of a million moments captured over the decades—the oldest going back to the early 20th century. There could have been many more, but many old-style glass plates and 4 x 5 inch negatives and their prints have been lost. Time and use, humidity, mold, bugs, fire, and water degrade and destroy.

And in the 21st century, digital photography and hard drive storage have placed ever larger quantities of images into archives. These too are fragile and must be maintained and backed up regularly. One computer crash or accidental click of a mouse and thousands of images could be wiped out. Any archive collection is only a portion of what it could have been. There is never a complete record.

Hawai'i 50: Five Decades of Photography, A Community Album covers the fifty years since Hawai'i became the fiftieth state. *Hawai'i 50* is the Honolulu community remembering itself via *Star-Bulletin* newspaper photographs.

Daily photo assignments accumulate to form community scrapbooks, reminders of times and places, records of events, and reference points for personal histories. They help us visualize, remember, and understand families, friends, and strangers in our hometowns and our world. Because we have seen the photographs, we remember.

These museums of images are a reminder of visual memories hidden in the storeroom of our minds which we rarely and vaguely perceive. Visual *déjà vu*. Fragments of images which stimulate the visual recall of entire periods of history.

News photographs live in our mind the way music does. The first notes of a song can bring back the melody of our past—our private past and our shared past. Photographs do the same. We see ourselves back in that time, in that place, the way we were.

And the way the world was. Think of the iconic images of the 20th century: the mushroom cloud of the first atomic bomb, the naked Vietnamese child running and screaming from

The Carnival at Aloha Tower Marketplace at sunset on New Years eve. December 31, 1996. (George F. Lee)

a napalm attack, that first photograph of Earth seen from space, and the first man walking on the moon.

The iconic images of Hawai'i create a different kind of portfolio. Forces of nature: volcanic eruptions, hurricanes, tsunamis, earthquakes. Forces of war: Pearl Harbor soldiers on leave. Forces of life: whales breaching. And, blessedly, life just being life: hula dancers moving like clouds passing across the mountains, monkeypod trees spreading their branches, surfers riding a gentle south swell. And local people living their local lives.

Nearly any photograph of old Hawai'i can evoke deep feelings for prewar landscapes and lifestyles. Even newcomers and strangers feel a sense of nostalgia, because we all seem to have a fascination with photographs from the past—anyone's past. In the future, these photographs from the past will be searched by historians, novelists, and filmmakers who are looking for bits of information, data, and explanations of previous eras and lifetimes.

Tragedies also form a large part of this great collective memory etched onto our mind's eye by the images recorded by photographers. There are the personal losses, deaths, and unbearable sufferings—intense situations where the photographer must be sensitive and hardened at the same time. He must be aggressive enough in the midst of the spot news to come back with the photograph on deadline, and sensitive enough to have concern and compassion for the victims.

Decade by decade, these newspaper photos show much of the gentleness of Hawai'i moving into the background. Life refocuses itself before our eyes—grainier, harder-edged, higher-speed. Every day, the population increases, more local landmark buildings and mom-and-pop businesses are bulldozed, their places on the skyline taken by standard-issue high-rises and chain stores. In reaction, the Native Hawaiian cultural renaissance has grown large and deeply political as well.

This rate of change accelerates. Memory and nostalgia become instant—or instantly forgotten. All the more reason to bring together in one book fifty years of our community memory in photographs.

In our collective memories, there is no single image that captures everything. As with words, thoughts, conversations, oral history, and films, persistence of vision takes many images and shapes them into a single iconic image. This is the image that we remember, that we believe, that we reference. It is our own personal truth and memory. Our scrapbook of history.

Franco Salmoiraghi

"The one place where all of these cycles of light and memory converge is 'history.' Photographs are fossils of light and memory, and photographs are the history of memory. That is my conclusion, for the time being."

–Daido Moriyama,
from his photographic
memoir, *Memories of a Dog*

Above: The Elite Men take to the ocean during the first segment of the Honolulu Triathlon Elite Men Division. April 16, 2005. (Jamm Aquino)

The Duke Statue Story

Photographers are usually interested in the moment that defines a situation or event. It may be the people, the light, the atmosphere, or the need to document what they are seeing. With the passage of time, these day-to-day moments can turn into history as photographs transcend time and the photographer's intentions.

Strolling and photographing along the Kalākaua Avenue beachside path in Waikīkī, I came to the statue of Duke Kahanamoku. Tourists were standing in front of him, talking on their cell phones, and waving. Looking around, I tried to understand what was happening. Were they being photographed for a commercial?

Scanning across Kalākaua to the hotel opposite, I expected to see a camera crew on the balcony. Nothing. The wavers kept waving, as people do when being photographed.

Searching the scene and looking over to the street light, there near the top I saw the camera—a stationary video eye recording every moment directly onto the Internet. The tourists on their cell phones were talking with their friends on the mainland while streaming video allowed them to be seen in Hawai'i with Duke and a famous Waikīkī sunset in the background.

The statue of Duke had to be modeled after photographs and not from life, I thought. He

departed January 22, 1968. His ashes floated on the waters of his Waikīkī. His statue, dedicated on August 24, 1990, the 100th anniversary of his birth, shows him with open arms—a gesture of warmth and welcome.

The elusive sculptor of Duke, Jan Gordon Fisher, responded to my attempts at contact. He confirmed that "Nadine Kahanamoku had many photographs in her collection, which the family shared with me. We cre-ated a storyboard, and I looked at them over and over, absorbing the energy of Duke from them."

I went looking for the photographs at the *Star-Bulletin* and other Honolulu repositories of visual history. At the Bishop Museum's photography archives, a place of rich community memory, I found photographs of Duke carefully categorized in folders from every period of his life: Sports, Celebrities, Swimming, Olympics. Thousands of images, including his wife Nadine's personal wedding album. There he was, standing as in the statue on a surfboard, in his element—straight, tall, and handsome, with arms wide open. And on his shoulders was a smiling young woman.

"Nadine's representative, Earl Pamai Tenn, demonstrated the stance they wanted, and later I saw that tandem surfing photograph," said Fisher. "It helped me to understand the spiritual part of the man. The family wanted the statue to convey Duke as an

ambassador to the world."

Duke was that, and the ocean was his element, as photographs of his life show over and over again: running through the surf, body surfing with his arms wide open, standing in the ocean five months before his death, as an older man in a 1967 *Star-Bulletin* photograph.

Duke was photographed thousands of times, and those images carry within them the history of twentieth century Waikīkī from the 1920s on—the beach, hotels, beachboys, tourists, and the dancers—revealing the elegance and warmth of the Hawaiian people. Duke, with his style and his smile, embodied all that history and aloha. The photographs, all those individual moments of visual data, many of them published in the daily newspapers of the era, went into the statue made by Fisher.

While looking through the photographs, I spoke with Bishop Museum Archives Collection Manager DeSoto Brown. "Photographs

contain information and emotion that is often obvious on the surface," he said. "But images need to be studied to see beyond that surface. Then its meaning becomes more immediate than similar information contained in words. Images touch us more quickly and easily, transporting us to the time and place they show."

Today, people from everywhere feel that deep Hawaiian energy in Duke when viewing his statue in Waikīkī. They stand in front of him to have their photograph taken with the icon no longer with us. Using traditional cameras with film, digital cameras, cell phone cameras, and the streaming video of the Internet, they travel back in time to Duke's era.

Watching the tourists frame themselves with Duke, I took photographs of them being photographed, in front of the statue inspired by photographs. Time may turn even this simple record into a historic photograph.

—Franco Salmoiraghi

Above: Duke Kahanamoku. "I'd like to go out and dive off the boat in deep water, or maybe go to the Wax Museum and get my big board and catch some of the waves out of Queen's Surf." August 21, 1967. (John Titchen)

CHAPTER ONE

1959
1969

Hawaiʻi becomes a State ❧ Nuclear testing on Johnston Island ❧ Hawaiʻi welcomes Frank Sinatra ❧ President Kennedy visits ❧ Elvis films *Blue Hawaii* ❧ Old Honolulu makes way for State Capi-tol ❧ Duke's Day in Waikīkī ❧ *Apollo 11* astronauts touch down ❧ Volcanic eruption overtakes Kapoho ❧ Wilson Tunnel dedi-cated ❧ La Pietra auction ❧ Fiftieth State Fair attracts youngsters

Opposite: The variety of rides at the 50th State Fair attracts youngsters; they especially enjoy the pint-sized roller coaster. July 10, 1960. (Amos Chun)
Above: This photo of news carrier Chester Kahapea selling copies of the Honolulu Star-Bulletin epitomizes the excitement of the day Hawaii becomes the last star on the US flag. August 21, 1959. (Albert Yamauchi)

Opposite page: 116,000 people sign a statehood petition in front of the Alexander Young Hotel on Bishop Street. 1954. (unknown)

Left: Coin divers wave aloha to passengers aboard the *President Cleveland* as she slowly sails out of Honolulu Harbor. Hundreds of passengers boarding the ship are members of excursion parties to see cherry blossoms in bloom in Japan. March 30, 1954. (unknown)

Top: The Royal Hawaiian Hotel. December 10, 1958. (unknown)

Above: Mary Kapeliela, left, and Bernadine Ah Nee, right, proudly model their new-style Trans-Pacific Airlines hostess uniforms. Georgette Collins, center, wears the old uniform. February 11, 1956. (TPA)

Above: Celebrating the Pineapple State.
March 1959. (unknown)

Right: Statehood celebration. Cars move
bumper to bumper through Waikiki.
1959. (Warren R. Roll)

Above: Statehood, Hawaii's most exciting story of 1959 was statehood, and here crowds are shown watching street dancers in Kalihi as the new state celebrated. Jan 1, 1960. (unknown)

Far left: The *Star-Bulletin*'s historic red, white and blue edition on March twelfth, the day that the Statehood Bill was passed, is held by Margaret Oshiro. April 14, 1959. (unknown)

Top: These boys find a highly practical use for the Board of Water Supply building's fountain on Beretania Street. July 4, 1959. (Jack Matsumoto)

Above left: The Kingston Trio belts out a number while taking in the beach at Waikiki. From left, the trio members are Nick Reynolds, Dave Guard and Bob Shane. October 25, 1958. (unknown)

Right: Workmen are putting finishing touches on the towering four-million-dollar Kaiser Foundation Medical Center on Ala Moana Boulevard. Every room will command a view of the sea or the mountains. The center is next to the Ala Wai Boat Harbor. September 25, 1958. (Warren R. Roll)

Left: It's "Steamer Day," and the twin-hulled catamarans in foreground are filled with people who have gone offport to wave their alohas to the arriving passengers. Aloha Tower, close to the ship's stack, is a world-famous gateway to Vacationland Hawaii. April 14, 1959. (unknown)

Below: View from Bishop Street, looking mauka toward Beretania Street. 1959. (Warren R. Roll)

Right: Narcisscus Festival. Linda Kwai Lan Tom, seated, was crowned Narcissus Queen and will reign during 1959. Her court, from left: Rhoda Tom, Carol Ann Ching, Laurita Char and Iwalani Lum-King. February 2, 1959. (Terry Luke)

Above: These seven young women will take part in the finals of the seventh annual Cherry Blossom Queen contest. From left, they are Joan H. Ogura, Flva T. Hamamoto, Lorraine R. Kirihara, June S. Fujikawa, Karen K. Yamaato, Jane M. Yamashita and Carole K. Ohtani. March 30, 1959. (unknown)

Right: Hawaii-Filipina Pageant. These four of the eighteen candidates are all students at the University of Hawaii. Left to right, they are Teresita Hilario, Leilani Fedalizo, Eleanor Nanod and Leticia Quintal. June 5, 1959. (unknown)

Above: Ala Moana Center under construction. April 1959. (unknown)

Left: Ala Moana Center Grand Opening. August 1959. (unknown)

Top: Aunt Jennie Wilson, widow of former Mayor Wilson, checks her household goods as she prepares to move out of her home. She particularly hates to part with the furniture, which the late Mayor made out of a huge koa log he found while building a road near Nahiku, Maui, in 1906. October 10, 1959. (unknown)

Above left: Maru's tuna catch at Kewalo Basin. April 21, 1959. (Warren R. Roll)

Above right: Tasting poi at a Luau. July 4, 1959. (Jack Matsumoto)

Top left: "We not worried," says Harriet Patterson, proprietor of lei booth number one on the Lagoon Drive approach to Honolulu Airport. Somehow a rumor got started that the new jet-age terminal would forsake the lei sellers. "They'll find a place for us," Harriet says confidently. October 30, 1959. (unknown)

Left: James Michener autographs *Hawaii* for Albertine Loomis. 1959. (Jack Matsumoto)

Right: Dan Inouye and his wife. The newly elected congressman leaves for Washington from Honolulu Airport. August 1959. (Albert Yamauchi)

Below: Fishing on the banks of the Ala Wai Canal. June 13, 1959. (Albert Yamauchi)

Left: Mr. and Mrs. Peter Lawford, left, and Sinatra, right. November 10, 1959. (Jack Matsumoto)

Left: A young Frank Sinatra looks very dapper singing in a white suit. October 1960. (unknown)

Above : United Air Lines employee Fredalina Coronas greets Pan American passenger Frank Sinatra on his arrival yesterday. September 25, 1960. (John Titchen)

Top: A portion of the seven thousand people at Duke's birthday party crowds around the former swimming champ. August 24, 1967. (John Titchen)

Above: Mayor (Neal) Blaisdell toasts Duke and hails his past triumphs at the Royal Hawaiian Hotel. Aug. 24, 1963. (John Titchen)

Right: Duke Kahanamoku waves "aloha" to more than five hundred people honoring him and his wife, Nadine. The event at the Waikiki Yacht Club climaxed an all-day "Duke's Day" at Waikiki. Governor William F. Quinn appointed Duke an honorary official greeter and ambassador-at-large for the state. August 20, 1962. (Albert Yamauchi)

Left: Duke with Nadine Kahanamoku. July 10, 1960. (Jack Matsumoto)

Below: Four champions pose with Duke. From left to right: Felipe Pomar, World

Meet Champion at Peru; George Downing; Mike Doyle, three-time Makaha Tandem Champ; and Fred Hemmings Jr., two-time Makaha Champ. December 13, 1965. (John Titchen)

Duke: The Ambassador of Aloha

An aptly named gentleman, Duke Kahanamoku possessed a courtly air that still radiates from his photographs. He always appeared at ease, whether dressed to the nines in suit and tie or swimming in the ocean that he loved so dearly. That ease before the cameras translated to his professional life as well. He was an athlete, appearing in three Olympic Games between the years 1912 and 1924, taking home three gold medals and two silver medals; and his surfing exhibitions in the first half of the twentieth century helped popularize the sport.

He was an actor, or rather an extra, but he did appear in *Mr. Roberts* with Henry Fonda and James Cagney. He was a restaurateur, an aloha ambassador, a raconteur, and the state's first international celebrity. In his lifetime, he met movie stars, presidents, and the Queen Mother, and it's a testament to his charm that they all came to him. After all, no visit to Hawai'i was complete until one had an audience with the Duke.

Duke Kahanamoku: "I'd like to go out and dive off the boat in deep water, or maybe go to the Wax Museum and get my big board and catch some of the waves out of Queen's Surf. A lot of Hawaiians have forgotten how to enjoy life."
August 21, 1967. (John Titchen)

Above left: When Vice President Nixon and his wife attended Sunday services at Kawaiahao Church, they were so impressed by Reverend Abraham K. Akaka that they invited him to be a guest minister in the White House and to bring along his choir. 1960. (unknown)

Above right: Michael J. Chun. 1960. (Jack Matsumoto)

Right: Candidates in the Miss Hawaii Filipina Contest honored by the Oahu Filipino Community Council at the Philippines Consulate include, clockwise from left: Adeline Perez, Gloria de la Cruz, Trinidad Orosco, Rosland Wagner, Jeanette Gallardo, Annie Orayan and Cynthia Domingo. March 27, 1960. (Warren R. Roll)

Left: After the tsunami, Hilo's business district, shown here, is destroyed, including the old American Factors building and the Hilo Theatre. The large building with the white roof at the lower right is the Palace Theatre. 1960. (Albert Yamauchi)

Below left: Bent parking meters show the power of tidal waves that struck downtown Hilo in 1960. The two-inch pipe is from the Bayfront Highway. 1960. (Terry Luke)

Below right: This volcanic eruption eventually overtook the Big Island town of Kapoho. January 1960. (Terry Luke)

Right: HPD Lieutenant Takeo Sato leads Sergeants Gus Anderson and Walter Dods down the inspection line as the second watch prepares to go on duty. January 17, 1960. (unknown)

Above: Bobby Ah Choy surfing on Kalakaua Avenue after the 1960 tsunami. 1960. (Warren R. Roll)

Right: Makaha Beach. April 17, 1960. (unknown)

Top: Thousands of spectators line King Street in front of Kawaiahao Church to watch the hour-long parade that highlighted Kamehameha Day observances. June 12, 1960. (Warren R. Roll)

Above: Alex H. Brodie, former Hawaiian Pineapple Company cannery superintendent, is ready to fight for a seat on Hapco's board of directors. June 9, 1960. (unknown)

Left: Children join the campaign to promote Neal Blaisdell by wearing shorts. September 1960. (unknown)

Above right: Sergeant Larry Mehau drove Vice President Nixon's car when he and Mrs. Nixon toured Honolulu. Mehau is seated in a situation that most security officers dislike: surrounded by a crowd. September 11, 1960. (unknown)

Right: Arthur A. Rutledge sits in his office at Unity House after being reinstated as president of Local 5, Hotel and Restaurant Employees Union. He was suspended on May 24th for alleged mishandling of funds. July 23, 1960. (Albert Yamauchi)

Top: This is the KGMB staff that will present Channel 9 Newsroom. From left, Frank Valenti, Peter Burns, Wayne Collins and Bob Miller. December 31, 1960. (John Titchen)

Left: C.S. Wo and Son's premiere showing of their company's new line of furniture attracts large crowds at the firm's Kapiolani Boulevard store. November 30, 1960. (Jack Matsumoto)

Above: Island homebuilder Joe Pao displays scale models of his proposed "twin homes," which would house two families under one roof. December 1960. (Amos Chun)

Below: Elvis Presley answers questions during a press conference attended mainly by representatives of high school papers. March 1961. (John Titchen)

Right: Tom Moffatt, Honolulu disc jockey, greets Elvis Presley as he arrives at Honolulu Airport for the filming of *Girls! Girls! Girls!*. April 1962. (Terry Luke)

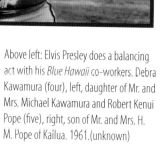

Above left: Elvis Presley does a balancing act with his *Blue Hawaii* co-workers. Debra Kawamura (four), left, daughter of Mr. and Mrs. Michael Kawamura and Robert Kenui Pope (five), right, son of Mr. and Mrs. H. M. Pope of Kailua. 1961.(unknown)

Above: Elvis Presley relaxes during a shooting of his horseback-riding scene. He chats with Charles O'Curran, choreographer for *Blue Hawaii,* who is scraping mud off his shoe. 1961. (unknown)

Top: Honolulu Iron Works in Kakaako. July 24, 1961. (unknown)

Above: Chinn Ho. 1961. (Warren R. Roll)

Left: Harry Weinberg, Honolulu Rapid Transit board chairman, listens intently at the Public Utilities Commission hearing. In the background is James K. Woolsey Jr., a director of H.R.T. March 20, 1961. (Jack Matsumoto)

Top: A panoramic view of Wailuku, the civic center of Maui, located at the base of the rugged West Maui Mountain. On the slopes are fields of sugar cane. Iao Valley opens to the center right—a scenic must for visitors of Maui. Highest peak of the West Maui Mountain is Mt. Puku at 5,788 feet. 1962. (Nobu Ianiguchi)

Above left: A man looks down from the site of the Sheraton Kaanapali towards Lahaina. In the background is the stack of Pioneer Mill. September 28, 1961. (Warren R. Roll)

Above: An old man, bent with age, in a Lahaina alley. September 28, 1961. (Warren R. Roll)

Left: Mrs. Hannah K. Niau, one of Niihau's two schoolteachers, and some of her pupils. Governor William F. Quinn inspected the school during his visit to the island. Classes are conducted in English, but few Niihauans speak the language well because Hawaiian is used at home. October 1961. (Jim Heckman)

Above: Niihau women don their brightest dresses for the holiday declared for the Governor's visit. They listen as Quinn says he'll help with any problems they may have. October 1961. (Jim Heckman)

Top: Niihau residents turn out in force at the island's only church to see Governor William F. Quinn and his party. October 1961. (Jim Heckman)

Below: A customer buys reindeer tendons in the Bo Sau Tong herb shop in the Aala Triangle area. May 30, 1961. (unknown)

Right: A woman plods down a junk-filled alleyway in the Aala Triangle area, one of the city's most crowded districts. May 30, 1961. (Warren R. Roll)

Above: Structures such as these stretch throughout the Aala Triangle. May 15, 1961. (Terry Luke)

Above: The Library of Hawaii has long recognized the value of its Bookmobile Division, a long and mobile arm of the library, which brings comradeship as well as books to Oahu's countryfolk. March 23, 1961. (John Titchen)

Left: The new sporting goods department of the Wigwam Department Stores holds an auspicious opening. New merchandise arrives everyday to maintain the minimum one-hundred-thousand-dollar inventory. May 1, 1961. (Jack Matsumoto)

Above: Aunt Jennie Wilson cuts a red carnation lei at the Wilson Tunnel dedication ceremonies. With her are, left to right, Cordeiro, Lieutenant Governor Kealoha, Mayor Blaisdell and Frank W. Finlayson. August 6, 1961. (John Titchen)

Above right: Thurston Twigg-Smith. 1962. (Albert Yamauchi)

Right: La Ronde Restaurant, a revolving restaurant atop Ala Moana Building. December 19, 1961. (Albert Yamauchi)

Left: Queen Stephanie Loo of the Narcissus Festival is shown (center) with her court. From left, they are Miss Tai, Miss Lau, Miss Young and Miss Yap. February 3, 1961. (Don Nelson)

Below left: Four of fifteen Cherry Blossom Queen candidates are recognizable in this picture taken at the Ala Moana Center. Standing on an escalator, from top to bottom, are Marjorie Aoyagi, Glenda Takaoka, Corinne Torii and Carole Dale Kuwahara. March 20, 1962. (Albert Yamauchi)

Below: The Miss Hawaii Pageant is one of the main attractions of the 50th State Fair. Among the many competitors are, from left: Bebee Gerard, Susan Molina, and Lynn Howell. June 27, 1962. (Ray Tierney)

Above: The city bought ten feet of this strip of land bordering Manoa Road from Joe Pao. Pao's Manoa Gardens subdivision is seen in the background. June 1962. (unknown)

Right: Construction of Honolulu's $4.6 million War Memorial Municipal Auditorium on the site of the Old Plantation, the former Ward property. June 28, 1962. (John Titchen)

Above: Several new churches border Kailua Road with the Nuuanu Pali in the background. Pohakupu subdivision is to the left, while beyond the churches to the right is Kawainui Swamp. Truesdale developers are proposing to construct a private housing subdivision in the swamp. April 15, 1962. (unknown)

Left: The Kailua Drive-In Theatre sign is put in place overlooking Pali Highway. The theatre's owners originally planned a five-hundred-square-foot sign for this site, but it was reduced to three-hundred-square-feet after the Lani-Kailua Outdoor Circle urged the City Council to pass an ordinance limiting the size of signs for drive-in theatres. November 17, 1964. (Albert Yamauchi)

Above left: President Kennedy in Hawaii. 1963. (unknown)

Above: An undated photo of U.S. Senator John F. Kennedy addressing a group on Maui. To the right is Gov. John Burns and to the left, Lt. Gov. William Richardson. (unknown)

Left: President Kennedy looks at the wreckage of the USS *Arizona* with, from left, Admiral Harry D. Felt, Senator Daniel K. Inouye, Governor John A. Burns, Representative Spark M. Matsunaga and Admiral John H. Sides. 1963. (unknown)

Opposite page: Top: Just before the nuclear test on Johnston Island. Below: Just after. July 8, 1962. (Warren R. Roll)

Above: Waikiki before the Outrigger Hotel. At left is the Moana Surfrider; at right is the Royal Hawaiian. 1963. (Warren R. Roll)

Right: The Nuuanu Y.M.C.A. moved out of its old home at Fort and Vineyard Streets after forty-five years. August 13, 1963. (Albert Yamauchi)

Above left: Leis like these held by Maile Lee will cost less at the airport stands during Aloha Week. Members of the Airport Lei Sellers Association decided to have reduced rates on their flowers as their contribution to the spirit of aloha. October 18, 1962. (Warren R. Roll)

Above: Beatle Ringo Starr is greeted at Honolulu International Airport. June 1964. (Terry Luke)

Left: A tourist is greeted at Honolulu International Airport with an orchid and pineapple juice. May 13, 1964. (Warren R. Roll)

Right: Norman C. Adams, left, and Joseph M. Long stand in front of their new store in the Waialae Shopping Center. August 15, 1963. (Albert Yamauchi)

Below: The McInerny building at Fort and Merchant Streets. October 5, 1964. (Terry Luke)

Above: These old Honolulu landmarks disappear to make way for the State Capitol. At left, from top to bottom are the Schulman Carriage building, a doctor's building and the Armory next to Iolani Barracks. At top right is the former Better Brands building, which houses the Hawaiian Government Employee's Association, and, below that, cottages between Punchbowl Street and the Barracks. May 1, 1964. (Terry Luke)

Left: A slight drizzle provides the traditional Hawaiian blessing as Governor John A. Burns and other officials conduct the ground-breaking ceremonies of the State Capitol on the former site of Iolani Barracks. November 10, 1965. (Warren R. Roll)

Above: Martin Denny plays at Duke Kahanamoku's. 1964. (unknown)

Right: The Gines family poses in front of their home at Poamoho Camp in Wahiawa, where they lived for seven years after Brigida Gines and her children emigrated from the Philippines. Ignacio Gines, next to his wife, came to Hawaii in 1946 and was a contract welder with Del Monte. From left to right, the children are: twins Shirley and Larry, and youngest Genevieve. 1964. (unknown)

Above left: Jean Charlot is a world-renowned artist, author, and colleague of the late Diego Rivera. A book of his plays makes its first appearance this year. March 28, 1964. (Warren R. Roll)

Above: Kenji Osano, Japanese financier and owner of the Moana Surfrider and Princess Kaiulani hotels. February 11, 1964. (John Titchen)

Left: Auctioneer Moe Lipton points out Mrs. Walter F. Dillingham's engraved initials on the bottom of a Georgian silver creamer to Mrs. Lily Center in the dining room of La Pietra. More than 2,600 items, such as these antique furnishings and art objects, are on public view in order to give interested buyers a chance to see items to be auctioned. September 23, 1964. (Warren R. Roll)

Above: Thomas Ponce Gill, or Tom Gill, Hawaii legislator (left), and US President Lyndon Baines Johnson. 1964. (unknown)

Above right: John Henry Felix, thirty-three pounds lighter because of the Governors' Conference, contemplates an array of food at a luau for the chief executives. June 1964. (Jack Matsumoto)

Right: Congressman Spark M. Matsunaga and his wife, Helene Matsunaga, reqister jubilation. He was re-elected to the U.S. House by a comfortable majority. November 3, 1964. (John Titchen)

Above left: Representative Patsy Mink with husband Jack. November 14, 1964. (Jack Matsumoto)

Far left: Samuel P. King. December 26, 1969. (Warren R. Roll)

Left: New Concept-Frank Fasi shows how a privately-developed stadium complex might look at Halawa. The model includes a round stadium, shopping center facilities and high-rise apartments. October 11, 1968. (Albert Yamauchi)

Above: Molii Fishpond at Kualoa Point, the north end of Kaneohe Bay. February 20, 1964. (John Titchen)

Right: Heeia fishpond, near Kahaluu. February 20, 1964. (John Titchen)

Left: A peek at the forthcoming view of Windward bays and peaks is an advantage the helicopter passengers had over earthbound travelers on Pali Highway. February 20, 1964. (John Titchen)

Below: Aerial view of the Kewalo Basin. 1965. (John Titchen)

Right: Sunday picnickers can't read signs at Kapiolani Park. The site is that of the old stables, and the land is being prepared as a park area. July 29, 1964. (John Titchen)

Below: Patrolman Daniel Cuban keeps one foot on gunman Otto Hillen outside the Moiliili Star Supermarket. Policemen at bottom left and right are weeping from tear gas. November 21, 1964. (Warren R. Roll)

Below right: Alfred S. Los Banos, formerly of the 5th Regimental Combat Team, inspects a map illustrating the Korean conflict. He was wounded by enemy fire on August 14, 1956, at Sabok San Mountain. August 12, 1964. (John Titchen)

Left: Activity is furious when the fishermen are working an aku school. September 29, 1965. (unknown)

Below: The Dole Pineapple stand near Wahiawa is getting a new look. The weather-beaten, white frame building is being torn down to be replaced by a seventy-thousand-dollar installation that includes an ultra-modern two-story building, lookout, park, museum and increased parking facilities. January 8, 1965. (Terry Luke)

Above : For her role in *The Typist*, Bette Midler strode onto the stage of the Kennedy Theatre, plunked herself down in front of a dilapidated typewriter, and typed and talked herself into the local theatre scene. March 4, 1965. (Warren R. Roll)

Above right: In her hula dancing, Iolani Luahine exudes quality, and even persons who have no understanding of her art recognize immediately that they are witnessing greatness. October 7, 1965. (Albert Yamauchi)

Right: Lei queen and court. From left: Miss Nina M. Lorenzo; Mrs. Carmen K. L. Maluo; Mrs. Geraldine K.V. Johnansen; Mrs. Nani Kapu Chan, lei queen; Mrs. Claire L. Check and Mrs. Ululani R. Daguay. One other court member was absent due to measles; she is Mrs. Antionette L. Lee. April 21, 1965. (John Titchen)

Above left: The Waikiki Biltmore towers over passing cars on Kalakaua Avenue. December 13, 1965. (Warren R. Roll)

Above: At the Farm Fair, Governor John A. Burns displays obvious relish as he prepares to bite into a juicy tomato. Clarence Ching's tomatoes were judged best in the produce show and won the Governor's trophy. June 16, 1966. (John Titchen)

Left: New beach pants are worn by, from left: Mark Buck, Barry Pritchard, Russell Starr, and Brant Ackerman. April 1965. (unknown)

Right: These fifteen Nisei girls compete for the 1967 Cherry Blossom Queen title at the Civic Auditorium. Left to right: Gerraine Maehara, Carol Arita, Sharon Ohta, Cynthia Aoki, Christine Suzuki, Cindy Shigeno, Gwen Nishizawa, Barbara Higashi, Ginger Matsumoto, Shiela Shimizu, Karen Kameda, Lynette Nishioka, Audrey Nakagaki, Judey Katayama and Sonia Asayama. January 31, 1967. (Jack Matsumoto)

Above: One of the most characteristic sounds of Hawaiian music, the moaning sigh of the steel guitar, is fading away. "The kids think Hawaiian music is a drag," says Barney Isaacs, a Hawaiian-Chinese who, at forty-two years of age, is part of what may be the last generation of steel guitarists. "They want to play rock 'n roll." December 24, 1966. (Albert Yamauchi)

Right: Songwriter Johnny Almeida (Pua's dad) celebrates his seventy-third birthday. Although sightless since he was seven days old, Johnny Almeida estimates that he has composed music and words to more than 250 songs. The flower is a persistent theme in the music and life of Almeida, who was born while his mother was in the Honolulu woods gathering maile for leis. May 25, 1967. (Jack Matsumoto)

Left: Siloama Church. Kalaupapa, Molokai. 1967. (Warren R. Roll)

Below: Sand Island. July 28, 1967. (John Titchen)

Right: The five trustees of the Bernice P. Bishop Estate, Hawaii's largest landed estate, meet in the boardroom of the Princess Pauahi Building in Kakaako. Left to right are Atherton Richards, Frank E. Midkiff, Edwin P. Murray, Herbert K. Keppeler and Richard Lyman, Jr. On the wall behind them are portraits of Princess Bernice Pauahi Bishop, whose will established the estate, and her husband, Charles Reed Bishop. March 4, 1967. (unknown)

Below: Harold Sakata, also known as Tosh Togo. He played Oddjob in Goldfinger, which came out in 1964. May 1967. (Jack Matsumoto)

Below right: University of Hawaii students, objecting to their large-sized classes in the Varsity Theater, picketed the theater. October 27, 1967. (John Titchen)

Left: One way to beat the heat is to get an old station wagon, roll the windows down and stick out your feet. August 15, 1967. (Bob Young)

Below left: Playing chess at Aala Park. March 29, 1967. (Albert Yamauchi)

Below: These Boy Scouts were among 1,500 members of the Aloha Council, Boy Scouts of America, who placed sixty thousand leis on graves in the National Memorial Cemetery of the Pacific in Punchbowl. From left, Makoto Hamilton, Bruce Bausell, and George Hee, all twelve years old and members of Troop 281. May 30, 1967. (unknown)

Right: Old buildings such as this one are commonplace in the Kalihi-Palama area of Honolulu. Such areas are targets for the Model Cities grant. November 15, 1967. (unknown)

Below: The crowds are big for the 1967 Makaha International Surfing Champion-ships. Many surfing fans camp at the beach for good vantage points. December 26, 1967. (Bob Young)

Above left: Guido Salmaggi with Duke Kahanamoku appeared together on Waikiki beach a few months before Duke died on January 22, 1968. Diamond Head is in the background. Both are shown sprinkling sand from Coney Island on Waikiki Beach. November 1967. (unknown)

Above: Chuck Leahey. January 11, 1968. (John Titchen)

Left: Wilfred Watanabe is giving lessons in surfing technique to many of the coeds who are starting classes at the University of Hawaii. June 18, 1968. (John Titchen)

Above: Don Ho (far left) unveils his new show at Duke Kahanamoku's. December 15, 1968. (Bob Young)

Right: A performer dances the hula at the Kodak Hula Show. 1969. (Warren R. Roll)

Far right: *Hawaii Five-O* star, Jack Lord. December 20, 1968. (Warren R. Roll)

Above left: Magdalena Raphael, Kona High School girl, picks coffee on her father's farm above Captain Cook. Phasing out the school coffee schedule may break the family labor pattern. February 7, 1968. (unknown)

Above: Richard Marks, a patient at the Kalaupapa settlement on Molokai, and his wife run a tour service of the settlement and Kalawao peninsula. October 18, 1968. (Warren R. Roll)

Left: Jack C. Reynolds, Governor John A. Burns, Jack W. Hall, Lowell S. Dillingham, and Arthur A. Rutledge join hands. April 1, 1968. (Albert Yamauchi)

Top: Looking from Ala Moana down Ward Avenue, where new storm drains are being installed, and the street is being widened to eighty feet. Utility poles will be removed and replaced by underground wiring. September 11, 1968. (Terry Luke)

Above left: Kailua branch of Holiday Mart. November 21, 1968. (Warren R. Roll)

Above: The Kapiolani Drive Inn will be demolished by bulldozers to make way for the Wailana condominium. July 10, 1968. (Albert Yamauchi)

Above left: After an afternoon on Waikiki Beach, California Governor Ronald Reagan searches for the key to his suite at the Ilikai Hotel. His wife, Nancy, waits more or less patiently. May 12, 1968. (Bob Young)

Above: Governor Ronald Reagan and his wife stay overnight in Hawaii before traveling on to the Philippines. The Governor and his family will represent President Nixon at the opening of a cultural center in Manila. September 5, 1969. (Warren R. Roll)

Left: Governor John A. Burns's children help him celebrate his sixtieth birthday at his Kailua home. The Governor's brother, Edward, and Mrs. Burns are on hand for the celebration with (from left) daughter Mary Beth Statts, Mrs. James (Lynette) Burns, Mrs. John A. Burns Jr., James and John Jr. The grandchildren are Meredith, three (left), and Brendan, twenty-two months, children of Lynette and James Burns, and Amanda, four, daughter of Jack Jr. March 30, 1969. (John Titchen)

Top left: Singer Danny Kaleikini looks slyly to his right. October 23, 1969. (Albert Yamauchi)

Top right: Neil Abercrombie, a thirty-one-year-old, flowing-haired University of Hawaii lecturer, who will teach in the American Studies Department, considers the "révolutionnaires" of the world as "not anti-establishment but pro-human." August 4, 1969. (Bob Young)

Above: The delicacies coveted by Hawaii's residents of Japanese descent for their traditional New Year's feast are very expensive. December 29, 1969. (Terry Luke)

Right: As cannery workers finish packing the cans, the tinned pineapple moves along mechanized chains to await juice and lids. July 25, 1969. (Bob Young)

Connecting All the Dots

The 1960s and 1970s were periods of seemingly endless expansion and construction in the islands. 1965 saw the construction of the State Capitol building, a project that helped transform the downtown area into the fast-paced business district that it is today. The late 60s and early '70s saw a boom in highway construction. The Lunalilo freeway, the H-3, and the Kalaniana'ole Highway were just a few of the roads projects that helped to connect the island of Oah'u. With all this new development, however, there was bound to be a price, a price that manifested itself in the sudden and sharp decline in a rural way of life. As the state modernized, the small town feel of the place was endangered. Country was less and less country as urban sprawl reached even the most remote corners of the state. Residents pushed back, launching grassroots endeavors to preserve a steadily vanishing way of life, but those efforts only stemmed the tide for a short while. The state continues its march towards development, as many of us wonder what we are losing in the process.

Top: The outbound lanes of the Waialae Overpass near completion, enabling motorists driving Koko Head on the Lunalilo Freeway to use them. June 5, 1969. (Warren R. Roll)

Above: Sleeping Giant-Work on the Kapiolani Interchange, which will move traffic smoothly between the one-mile Kaimuki stretch of Interstate freeway to the Lunalilo Freeway, should have been completed next week. But work came to a halt with the carpenter's strike. Highway officials estimate three weeks of work remain before the interchange can be opened to traffic. September 11, 1967. (John Titchen)

Above: Aerial view of Haleakala on Maui. January 28, 1969. (Warren R. Roll)

Right: Honolulu Stadium. December 23, 1969. (unknown)

The *Apollo 11* astronauts, Neil Armstrong,
Buzz Aldrin, Jr., and Michael Collins,
touch down in Hawaii in their mobile
quarantine facility. July 26, 1969.
(unknown)

CHAPTER TWO

1970 1979

Lucky You Live Hawai'i ❦ Sunshine Music Festival ❦ "Hippy Haven" Mākena Beach ❦ President Nixon visits ❦ *Hawaii 5-O* series ends ❦ Tūtū and their hats ❦ Stocking up on sashimi ❦ Kalama Valley ❦ Veteran hotelman Roy C. Kelley ❦ Mom-and-pop stores ❦ Emma and Hal ❦ Manapua Wagon ❦ Malasada Day ❦ *Hōkūle'a* ❦ Bette Midler returns ❦ All-star center Mufi Hanneman

Opposite: Hotel Street. How would a woman handle a policeman's job? February 4, 1974. (Bob Young)

Above: Bette Midler came to Honolulu on a tide of calculated tawdriness and whiplash vulgarity, a child of Aiea who made it in the big time, all by herself. This was her first appearance in her hometown as the Divine Miss M. September 6, 1973. (Bob Young)

Top: The old face of Kakaako is reflected in a family store on Queen Street. March 10, 1970. (Warren R. Roll)

Above left: Among those at the McKinley High School Class of 1924 reunion were, from left, Sen. Hiram L. Fong, Edward Himrod, Chinn Ho, and Associate Justice Masaji Marumoto. March 31, 1970. (Bob Young)

Above: A hat—and that was that so far as clothing was concerned for one youth who attended the Sunshine Music Festival. January 2, 1970. (Warren R. Roll)

Left: Ewa Beach. Ewa Sugar Mill. June 28, 1970. (Warren R. Roll)

Below left: The Chamber of Commerce of Hawaii has emblazoned "Lucky You Live Hawaii" posters across the sides of buses in Honolulu. Admiring the work by Pacific Sign and Decal are Ray Milici, left, a chamber director, and Hachiro Fujiyoshi. July 22, 1970. (Terry Luke)

Below: TV chairs at the Honolulu International Airport. 1970. (Terry Luke)

Top: An hour before the box-office at Honolulu Stadium opened to sell tickets for the Pacific Coast League playoffs. August 26, 1970. (Terry Luke)

Above left: Frank Fasi with Governor John A. Burns. September 1, 1970. (Albert Yamauchi)

Above: The Otani home may soon be available to the public. The City has taken possession of two of the more luxurious homes on Diamond Head as the first step in its park expansion plan. The City has deposited a total of $1.3 million in the court for the land. July 24, 1970. (John Titchen)

Top left: Bob Nash. October 16, 1971. (Albert Yamauchi)

Top right: Mufi Hannemann, 1971 ILH All-Star center, Leading Scorer, Most Valuable Player. 1971. (unknown)

Above left: It was a hot day, and nobody was interested in this woman's leis, which were more colorfully arranged than the merchandise in the window above her. So the lei seller put her head down for a mid-day nap. September 21, 1970. (Terry Luke)

Above: Representative Neil Abercrombie, who says that he is "the only serious candidate for U.S. Senate," is having a hard time proving it. Perhaps it is the faded flowered bell-bottom jeans and the Edwardian shirts he wears, or his hair that flows well below his shoulders. October 1, 1970. (John Titchen)

Top: Compare this rain-washed scene in Kaunakakai with crowded Oahu, and you may decide to move to the Friendly Island. January 20, 1971. (Denise Titchen)

Above left: Women have their place in life, singer Emma Veary said, as she sat in their Kahala beachfront home, which her husband, Hal Lewis, described as Grecian-Oriental-modern. Hal, also known as Akuhead Pupule, KGMB's controversial disc jockey, warned that his wife is very much against the women's liberation movement. December 3, 1970. (Albert Yamauchi)

Above: Proprietor Harry Hasegawa, of the Hasegawa General Store on Maui, hangs hula-hoops in his well-stocked general store, which, as the song says, carries "baseball bats, paniolo hats, sunburn cream and the latest magazines." October 17, 1970. (Keith Haugen)

Above: Work on the Kailua interchange of the H-3 freeway is moving closer to completion. Mokapu Boulevard comes from lower right of photo underneath the freeway. February 18, 1971. (Warren R. Roll)

Left: The Mokapu interchange on the H-3 freeway includes the normal "spaghetti" of connecting roads found at all freeway junctions. Kaneohe Bay Drive passes under the freeway and along a housing subdivision. May 15, 1972. (Warren R. Roll)

Above: Edwin "Sonny" Chillingworth, a singer-guitarist who performs at the Blue Dolphin in the Outrigger hotel, is one of the artists to appear at the Hawaiian Music Foundation's second slack-key guitar concert. December 21, 1971. (Dick Schmidt)

Above right: Leonard's Bakery baker Janjo Nakamoto, left, and Mrs. Helen Takahara had to fill a huge order of an island favorite. It's Malasada Day, a traditional Portuguese community event observed on the day before Ash Wednesday. February 22, 1971. (Albert Yamauchi)

Right: Manapua Wagon. February 8, 1971. (unknown)

Left: Pineapple workers coming back from the fields to Whitmore Village. March 2, 1971. (John Titchen)

Below right: Five of these girls will be selected in the Oahu Filipina beauty finals for the state finals to select a Hawaii-Filipina Queen. Left to right, Debbie Cabiles, Julia Escalona, Frances Ballangao, Gail Quipotla, Dancette Villamor, Thelma Supnet, Evangeline Salomon, and Marlene DeVera. May 1, 1971. (Albert Yamauchi)

Above: There's not much room in the bookmobile when the choosing and perusing begins. In a month the bookmobile visited sixty-nine Windward communities. February 4, 1971. (unknown)

Right: Kalakaua Avenue. October 19, 1971. (Albert Yamauchi)

Below right: Mrs. Mary Lou Kekuewa, historian of the Queen Emma Hawaiian Civic Club, demonstrates the art of feather lei making. June 1, 1972. (Terry Luke)

Below: On Sam Sanford's KGU show, Jim Leahey puts on his character of Rosie Cabral and reports on the wrestling matches at the Honolulu International Center. February 21, 1972. (Dick Schmidt)

A Legend in Our Time

He was a legend, a country boy from the Windward side of O'ahu who went on to become one of the most visible figures in the Hawai'i entertainment business. It didn't start out that way. Donald Tai Loy Ho was going to be a sociologist (he earned a bachelor's degree in the discipline from the University of Hawai'i at Mānoa in 1953) or maybe a pilot (he flew jets for the United States Air Force in the mid-1950s). It wasn't until he left the Air Force in 1959 and began singing in his mother's nightclub, the legendary Honey's, that he caught the show-biz bug and his celebrity began to grow. Then came the standing gig at Duke Kahanamoku's club, the record deal, the tours, the television appearances (*The Brady Bunch* most famously) and his top ten hit that would forever be his signature song: "Tiny Bubbles." In later years, Ho stopped touring and settled into a regular gig, playing to packed audiences at the Waikīkī Beachcomber. It seemed that he would always be around, wearing his satin jacket and cap, sitting behind the keyboard, bantering with tourists. And then he was gone. Don Ho died on April 14, 2007. His memorial service, held in Waikīkī a few weeks later, was thronged with people mourning the man and the era that had passed with him.

Top: Don Ho and friends. April 10, 1972. (Bob Young)

Above left: Don and members of his show business family. Sam Kapu, left. Angel Pablo in hat. Patty Swalley and Tokyo Joe. 1976. (Unknown))

Above right: Reading congratulatory telegrams on opening night at the Polynesian Palace. Sept. 16, 1970. (Bob Young)

Right: Newly formed Society of Hawaii's Entertainers presents "Waikiki —The Way it Was" at the Hilton Hawaiian Village. Reminiscing are society members, from left, Jack and Cha Thompson, Don Ho and Dick Jensen. April 29, 1979. (John Titchen)

Right: Kalama Valley demonstration. Bishop Estate. Kokua Hawaii. May 11, 1971. (Warren R. Roll)

Below: Kokua Hawaii pickets the state court building while, inside, a former Kalama Valley resident fights to regain entry to his valley home. The dead pig signs refer to the pigs, owned by former Kalama resident George Santos, that have died since they were moved from the valley. May 24, 1971. (Terry Luke)

Above left: Shoppers throng the open air Oahu fish market in Chinatown, stocking up on sashimi for New Year's celebrations. Prices were running as high as eight dollars a pound for ahi. December 30, 1971. (Terry Luke)

Left: On Wednesday the Ala Wai canal in Waikiki was a mirror. The trade winds have stopped. And when they stop, it's a sign that bad weather is ahead. February 2, 1972. (Warren R. Roll)

Above: Jesse Kuhaulua. 1972. (unknown)

Above right: Sumo star Jesse Kuhaulua took on some of his childhood pals as part of the activities welcoming the champion back to his home island of Maui. Charlie Arruda, the 260-pounder on the right, grimaced and groaned but could not budge Takamiyama, Jesse's alias in Japan. August 24, 1972. (Albert Yamauchi)

Right: Transients living on Maui's Makena Beach have been evicted, and their homes will be razed. Officials said lack of proper sanitation facilities at "Hippie Haven" poses a health hazard to nearby communities. April 20, 1972. (unknown)

Below: Even if this speed limit sign doesn't slow you down, it catches your eye. The sign is on Waikoloa Drive in the Waikoloa development about ten miles from Waimea. March 5, 1973. (Bob Young)

Ota Camp. Above Left: Modesto Baisac's family. Left: Just cruising around. April 2, 1972. (John Titchen)

Right: Reservoir No. 4 in Nuuanu is open for fishing on weekends. April 7, 1972. (Terry Luke)

Below: Clare Boothe Luce. December 27, 1972. (Ron Edmonds)

Below right: Mary K. Pukui, seventy-seven, at a luau in Ka'u where she was born and raised. May 1, 1972. (unknown)

Top: The Oceania, a 1,200-ton steel craft that will become Hawaii's first floating restaurant, was towed into Honolulu Harbor and docked at Pier 6 after a six-week Pacific Ocean crossing from Hong Kong. August 29, 1972. (John Titchen)

Above left: Applauding a fund donation for five hundred dollars for the Kui Lee Cancer Fund from Hilton Hotels: City Auditoriums Director Matt Esposito, RCA Records President Rocco Laginestre, Elvis Presley, and Nani Lee. Hilton Vice President Don Madsen made the presentation. November 1972. (John Titchen)

Above: State Senator D.G. Andy Anderson seems nonchalant after losing the mayor race to Mayor Frank F. Fasi. November 7, 1972. (Ron Edmonds)

Right: President Richard M. Nixon in Hawaii. August 30, 1972. (Bob Young)

Below right: The Wigwam store in Dilligham Plaza sports a new name as the chain's eight Hawaii stores begin to conform with the title of the Oakland-based corporate parents, PayLess Drug Stores Inc. September 9, 1973. (John Titchen)

Top left: Hilo Hattie is greeted with a kiss by Hawaii Calls host Danny Kaleikini. August 27, 1973. (Terry Luke)

Top right: A lifetime member of the Musicians Union, Senator Daniel K. Inouye plays his version of "Danny Boy" as the closing act of his one-hundred-dollar-a-plate fundraiser. August 3, 1973. (Bob Young)

Above left: Bette Midler—the Divine Miss M.—is back home in Hawaii. Former resident of Halawa Housing, Radford High class of '64 and ex-cannery worker, is getting ready for a pair of concerts at Honolulu Concert Theater. September 2, 1973. (Bob Young)

Above: Sunday Manoa. From left, Roland Cazimero, Peter Moon and Robert Cazimero. February 18, 1973. (Ron Edmonds)

Right: Signs like this one become popular as gasoline companies are forced to make further cuts in the amounts supplied to service stations. Rodney Kahn of Kahn's Service feels "people will adjust to the situation." November 26, 1973. (Ron Edmonds)

Below: "Retired" veteran hotelman Roy C. Kelley, right, and his son Richard Kelley, left, outside the newest Kelley Hotel, the 356-room Waikiki Village. February 14, 1974. (John Titchen)

Below right: A group of Natatorium supporters enjoy a swim in the Waikiki waters that won a reprieve from destruction. October 3, 1973. (John Titchen)

Above: The tutus, the grandmothers, stroll out to the center of the lawn, broad-brimmed hats shading their faces. One has a spray of anthuriums, large enough for a respectable centerpiece, attached to the band of her hat. The tutus personify old Hawaii and a passing graciousness. What a glorious surprise to find them at the Kodak Hula Show, which in name, at least, sounds as if it is among the most commercial of all commercial things connected with Hawaiian tourism. April 12, 1974. (unknown)

Left: Bernice Ramos gives a haircut to her father, Angel. Rose, Angel's wife, is on the far left. 1974. (Dennis Oda)

Above: Salt Lake, midway in fill operations in 1974. The filling-in of Salt Lake and construction of a twenty-seven-hole golf course have brought screams from environmental groups and support from golfing enthusiasts. January 18, 1974. (Warren R. Roll)

Right: Honolulu International Airport Runway. Protective structure in foreground and 36" dredge in the upper right hand corner, dredging circulation channel. April 1974. (Harvey E. Mohler)

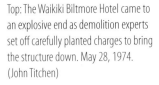

Top: The Waikiki Biltmore Hotel came to an explosive end as demolition experts set off carefully planted charges to bring the structure down. May 28, 1974. (John Titchen)

Above left: The word got around to fishermen in a hurry that a lot of halalu were being caught at Honolulu harbor. It was elbow to elbow on the wall across from the Hawaiian Electric plant on Nimitz Highway. One fisherman theorized that the fish, baby akule, were chased close to shore by a school of tuna. August 13, 1974. (John Titchen)

Above: George B. Rosete grooms one of his roosters at the gamecock exhibits at the State Farm Fair. June 30, 1974. (John Titchen)

Right: The State Harbors Division has ordered boat rental operators on the Ala Wai canal to remove this sign, which apparently violates the city sign ordinance. September 10, 1974. (Bob Young)

Below: Punchbowl. Nehe Lane. October 4, 1974. (Ken Sakamoto)

Below right: Randolph Crossley, Republican candidate for governor, and his Democratic opponent, Acting Governor George R. Ariyoshi, appear together on KITV-TV's Word 4 Word program. KITV news director Don Rockwell, left, is the moderator. November 1, 1974. (Ken Sakamoto)

Above left: Ron Edmonds, staff photographer of the *Honolulu Star-Bulletin*, was named among top winners in three categories in the annual Associated Press photo and news writing contests. Edmonds's photograph, entitled "Don't Get Excited" and showing a distraught teenager standing on the ledge of the Family Court Building with a judge talking to her, won second place in the metropolitan news division. February 3, 1975. (Ron Edmonds)

Above: David Akana Espinda Jr. sat in front of the television cameras, screwed up his face, made an "O" with his thumb and middle finger and said: "Shaka Brah!" Almost overnight it caught on, not only as a popular saying but also as a trademark for him and his television show. Espinda, sixty-two, is better known as Lippy and called the "king of pidgin." April 25, 1975. (Warren R. Roll)

Left: Citizens hoping to stop H-3 from being built through Moanalua Valley massed at the Capitol to voice their dissent. March 20, 1975. (Bob Young)

Above: Two young women walk on cracked sidewalks in Haleiwa. Old men, idle, sit and watch. October 1975. (John Titchen)

Above right: Mrs. Kamikichi Higa mends the awning in front of her family store on Kalihi Street. She and her husband first opened the store in March 1941. January 24, 1975. (Ken Sakamoto)

Right: Entering Moiliili is like wandering into an incongruous wonderland. Look here, there and everywhere because you'll find the most unexpected things in the most unexpected places. December 15, 1975. (John Titchen)

Top: Kaimuki. Looking ewa down Waialae Avenue. October 14, 1975. (Ron Edmonds)

Above left: Dai'ei. Second floor snack shop. 1975. (Warren R. Roll)

Above: One of the most beautiful teahouses is Nuuanu Onsen, which comes closest to capturing the atmosphere of the teahouse in Japan. Two of the older teahouses recently have been razed to make way for condominiums and townhouses. June 26, 1975. (Bob Young)

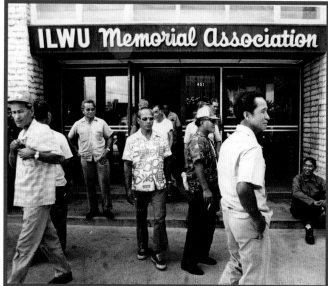

Above: Aerial view of Aloha Stadium. The new Aloha Stadium was moved into the baseball configuration with home plate at the top of the aerial photo. June 30, 1975. (Warren R. Roll)

Right: International Longshore and Warehouse Union members leave the union hall on Atkinson Drive after a briefing on the status of Hawaii longshore contract talks. September 3, 1975. (Terry Luke)

Top: Genoa Keawe and her group at Aloha Grill. A spectator plays the spoons at far left. October 23, 1975. (Bob Young)

Left: Marchers leave River Street to protest pending city evictions in the Chinatown area. November 24, 1975. (John Titchen)

Above: Pineapple fields. Vegetables, rice, and fish for lunch. August 20, 1976. (Ron Edmonds)

Hawaiian Pride

It began with musicians, artists like Gabby Pahinui and the Sons of Hawai'i, whose traditional Hawaiian recordings had been rediscovered by a new generation of Hawaiians, curious about their past. Then it spread to voyaging, cultural awareness, the emergence of Hawai'i Creole English, or Pidgin, in literature, and politics. Suddenly, native Hawaiians, whose culture and language had been marginalized for two centuries, were making their presence known. Various sovereignty movements arose, calling for the reestablishment of the Kingdom of Hawai'i, and leaders rose with it—Haunani Kay Trask, Dennis "Bumpy" Kanahele, and George Helm, to name a few. While the re-emergence of Hawaiian pride was welcomed by many, not all looked upon it positively. (The United States Navy weren't too pleased when George Helm led a group of protestors to Kaho'olawe, which at the time was used for target practice for Navy guns.) Still the Renaissance signaled a sea change in local thinking and culture that still reverberates many years later.

Above: George Helm is concerned about the loss of Hawaiian lifestyles, not just his own, but the lifestyles he feels so important to all Hawaiians. And, at the expense of being labeled a radical, activist or trouble-maker, he is doing something about it. Helm has been active-along with Walter Ritte Jr., Dr. Emmett Aluli and others-in the "invasion" of Kahoolawe, the Hui Aloha marches to gain public access to Molokai beaches and such causes as the plights of the residents of Waiahole-Waikane and Heeia-Kea. June 23, 1976. (John Titchen)

Top: Gabby Pahinui. 1975. (Bob Young)   Above: Kapono and Keola Beamer.
                                            January 14, 1975. (Bob Young)

Above: Three local acts for second annual Hawaii Contemporary Music Festival on March 20, 1977, at the Blaisdell Arena. Olomana (left), Booga Booga (center three), and Brothers Cazimero (right). February 28, 1977. (Jerry Chong)

Left: Cecilio and Kapono sing in language the young understand. December 8, 1977. (Warren R. Roll)

Top left: A crater festival at the end of the tunnel. December 31, 1975. (Warren R. Roll)

Top right: The promoters of Diamond Head Crater festival say that Robert Kozminski, of Fire Productions, who financed the festival has left town with the profits, and they've asked the FBI to step in. Kozminski has not been seen since Friday after he collected the "extra money" from ticket offices. December 31, 1975. (John Titchen)

Above: Diamond Head. Crater festival. September 3, 1978. (Bob Young)

Left: The fate of Japan's economy is also the fate of a chunk of Hawaii's visitor industry. Japanese tourists, like these arriving at Honolulu Airport, travel when their home economy is good and stay home when times are bad. March 17, 1976. (Warren R. Roll)

Below left: Boys' Day. Jason and his parents. April 26, 1976. (Terry Luke)

Below: Hari Kojima trying to sell an awa awa. August 25, 1976. (John Titchen)

Right: Campus guards carry a protester from the University of Hawaii's Bachman Hall and take him to a waiting police wagon. April 1, 1976. (Bob Young)

Below: University of Hawaii vice president Dewey Kim, standing in center in printed shirt, talks to supporters of threatened Ethnic Studies program in the foyer of Bachman Hall. December 1, 1976. (Ken Sakamoto)

Above: A valley of singing water on Kauai was the inspiration that gave the name Waioli to the Salvation Army's restaurant in Manoa Valley. The Waioli Tea Room is one of the oldest restaurants in Honolulu. July 13, 1976. (Ron Edmonds)

Above left: It's just like any other beautiful Hawaiian sunset, except that it is seen by fewer people. Watching it from the quiet, peaceful peninsula of Kalaupapa gives you a special feeling that makes a visit to this remote part of Molokai well worth the trip. August 29, 1976. (Ron Edmonds)

Above: Disc Jockey Ron Jacobs shows off his huge collection of t-shirts. September 20, 1976. (Ron Edmonds)

Left: Kaahumanu Society. June 1, 1976. (Warren R. Roll)

Right: Although Sam Ichinose has lost $135,000 over the past two years, the boxing promoter feels that he's on his way back—if not to the penthouse, at least not to the poorhouse. January 13, 1977. (Ken Sakamoto)

Below: Race organizer Carole Kai rests her hand on a perpetual trophy as she watches beds whiz by. January 23, 1977. (John Titchen)

Below right: Arthur Rutledge. January 15, 1977. (Ken Sakamoto)

Left: University President Fujio Matsuda speaks to the four thousand demonstrators gathered at the Capitol to protest planned cuts in the University system budget. March 4, 1977.
(Ken Sakamoto)

Below left: More than two thousand demonstrators near the State Capitol on Beretania Street join two thousand protestors from community colleges during their march from Manoa to protest planned cuts in the University of Hawaii budget. March 4, 1977. (Warren R. Roll)

Above: Walter Ritte Jr., in a malo, his daughter, and his wife, Loretta, in a kikepa, walk to the old federal building where Ritte is standing trial for allegedly trespassing on Kahoolawe. June 21, 1977. (Ron Edmonds)

Right: Critics of redevelopment plans for Chinatown fear that communal style living favored by the residents will be lost if the old buildings are replaced by high-rises. May 23, 1977. (Terry Luke)

Above: The press corps covering the bribery trail of Mayor Frank F. Fasi and Harry C.C. Chung gained a new member—former University of Hawaii football coach Larry Price. Price, who joined Radio K59 as vice president of public relations and publicity, provides daily "color" reports for Hal "Aku" Lewis on his morning program. August 2, 1977. (Terry Luke)

Above: Trustee Robert R. Rouse tells a crowd of about one thousand the details of the Kuilima Estates East condominium auction. March 6, 1977. (John Titchen)

Left: The Miss Hawaii Pageant means nervous waiting at rehearsals, and beauties in swimsuits during competition. June 6, 1977. (Terry Luke)

Below: Hotel Street scenes.
Left: May 23, 1977. Right: May 25, 1977.
(Terry Luke)

Below: Joggers and fisherman seem to have little in common except for the promenade along the Ala Wai. September 29, 1977. (Craig T. Kojima)

Right: The trail to the beach through thorny keawe trees at Kuilei Cliffs on Diamond Head looks like an obstacle course for the surfers, who head that way for the good waves. July 13, 1977. (John Titchen)

Above: Though they appear rundown, these houses on Leilehua Lane, just above the H-1 freeway at Punchbowl, are still occupied. December 13, 1977. (Craig T. Kojima)

Top: State Capitol. Exteriors. January 13, 1978. (Ron Edmonds)

Above: It looks like a street in an old plantation camp, but this scene was revealed when a lot on Halekauwila Street in the heart of the Kakaako district was cleared. It is between Koula and Ohe Streets. February 9, 1978. (John Titchen)

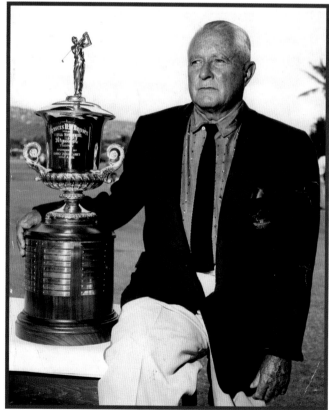

Top: Kamehameha School. The winning senior class of the song contest. March 17, 1978. (Bob Young)

Above left: Former legislator and golfer Francis I'i Brown, with the Manoa Cup. 1978. (unknown)

Above: John Penebacker with one-year-old daughter, Dawn. July 5, 1978. (unknown)

Pride of the Nation

Built at the height of the Hawaiian Renaissance by the Polynesian Voyaging Society, the canoe *Hōkūle'a* became a symbol of resurgent Hawaiian pride. It was a replica of a traditional Polynesian canoe, built to dispel the long-held belief that Polynesians had discovered the Hawaiian Islands by accident. During the canoe's first voyage, in 1976 to Tahiti, the crew members used no modern navigational instruments, relying instead on wayfinding, or navigating by the stars, winds, and currents. That first trip was a success and the crew returned as heroes, ushering in a new age of awareness of Hawaiian culture in the Islands. The second voyage, undertaken in 1978, began in tragedy as the canoe was swamped in the seas off Moloka'i. Crewmember Eddie Aikau was lost at sea when he attempted to paddle for rescue. That terrible moment could not stop the *Hōkūle'a*, which was still sailing as recently as 2007, spreading the word about Polynesian voyaging far and wide.

Above: *Hokule'a,* the double-hulled voyaging canoe, which Herb Kane designed. This year *Hokule'a* will duplicate, in reverse, the original Pacific migrations of the Polynesians which brought them to Hawaii more than 1,000 years ago. 1976. (unknown)

Top: The twin-hulls of the capsized *Hokule'a.* The crew of the Coast Guard cutter Cape Corwin helped to right the canoe, and the cutter took it in tow. March 18, 1978. (Ken Sakamoto)

Above: Eddie Aikau press conference. Henrietta and Pops (Solomon) Aikau sit in living room filled with surfing memorabilia won by sons Eddie and Clyde. March 22, 1978. (Warren R. Roll)

Right: Residents on state land on Sand Island enjoy a leisurely life of fishing and boating without rental problems. April 10, 1978. (Terry Luke)

Below: Pedicab drivers and operators arrive at City Hall. May 19, 1978. (Warren R. Roll)

Below right: Waikiki Beach is jammed as tourists and residents enjoy the July Fourth holiday by swimming, surfing, sunbathing, and watching Hawaiian canoe-racing events. July 4, 1978. (John Titchen)

"Goodbye, ol' girl . . ."

Top left: Rap Reiplinger. July 11, 1978. (Craig T. Kojima)

Top right: Andy Bumatai. December 6, 1978. (Warren R. Roll)

Far left: Loyal Garner. August 17, 1978. (Craig T. Kojima)

Left: Melveen Leed claims that as a teenager she was shy. That's difficult to believe after watching her burst on stage at the Ilikai's Canoe House, singing a tasty selection of pop tunes intermingled with her Molokai humor. September 21, 1978. (Albert Yamauchi)

Above: Pat Morita, who played Mona's husband and bartender at Mona's Bar. 1979. (Ken Sakamoto)

Above right: Waiahole protest. "Against Development Is What We Say. Waiahole Waikane Is Here To Stay." August 23, 1978. (Bob Young)

Right: Charles Reppun inspects tall taro, which will shrink to a size suitable for harvest. September 7, 1978. (Bob Young)

Above: Makaha Sons of Niihau at
Sky Gate Concert. March 7, 1979.
(Ken Sakamoto)

Left: Outrigger Canoe Club. The hau
terrace of the club dining room.
April 10, 1979. (John Titchen)

Right: Missing fox symbol of the Inari Shrine in Moiliili is being sought by a group that plans to move the structure to Waipahu. May 3, 1979. (unknown)

Below: Derek Tatsuno, a twenty-one-year-old junior at the University of Hawaii, holds a San Diego Padres' press book after he was drafted by the Padres in the second round of the Major League Baseball draft. Tatsuno is the only pitcher in collegiate baseball history to win twenty games in a season. June 5, 1979. (John Titchen)

Below right: Lunch wagon. June 27, 1979. (Ken Sakamoto)

Above left: Lieutenant Governor Jean King looks over some of the entries in her contest to select a design for Hawaii's 1981 license plate. July 23, 1979. (Warren R. Roll)

Above: Les Keiter, voice of the Hawaii Islanders, covered big-time sports for the New York Giants and New York radio stations. In his Mainland broadcasting days, Keiter covered Sonny Liston, and was with William Holden, John Wayne and Howard Cosell at the Patterson-Johansson fight on June 26, 1959. May 21, 1979. (Craig T. Kojima)

Left: A National Guard helicopter waits with rotors whirling in the Ainako area of Hilo, while police load marijuana confiscated from nearby brushland. June 27, 1979. (Craig T. Kojima)

Right: Kalihi is a community of mom-and-pop grocery stores and gold mines for antique hunters. August 14, 1979. (Ken Sakamoto)

Below: About 150 United Public Workers pickets march in front of the Prince Kuhio Federal Building as negotiators meet inside with a federal mediator. October 29, 1979. (Terry Luke)

Below right: Victor Fukata, operator of Emma Cab Co., uses his bags of trash accumulated during the United Public Workers' strike to make a statement against Iran and about his disappointment in the U.S. government's handling of the hostage situation. December 5, 1979. (Warren R. Roll)

Above left: Sponsor Joe DiPaulo of South Pasadena, California, and the director Fred Hemmings, right, decide to postpone the start of the women's surfing championship. Contestants Nancy Emerson, left, of Haiku, Maui, and Rell Sunn of Makaha were among those who concurred with the decision. December 17, 1979. (John Titchen)

Above: Rell Sunn demonstrating power and grace. December 19, 1979. (Ken Sakamoto)

Left: Kahoolawe access. September 14, 1979. (Warren R. Roll)

CHAPTER THREE

1980 1989

President and Nancy Reagan visit ❦ Tamashiro Fish Market ❦ Merrie Monarch ❦ Astronaut Ellison Onizuka ❦ Last rites for Gabby ❦ Hale‘iwa shave ice ❦ The Fabulous Five ❦ The Beamer clan ❦ Easter sunrise at Punchbowl ❦ Nainoa Thompson, *Hōkūle‘a* navigator ❦ Ghost storyteller Glen Grant ❦ Big Board Buddies ❦ Alexander Young Building comes down ❦ Jerry Santos wins Album of the Year ❦ Hulihuli chicken ❦ Armed Services YMCA for sale ❦ Gone fishing

Opposite page: Rell Sunn, "The Queen of Makaha." May 23, 1983. (Dennis Oda) Above: Aloha Airlines Flight 243 Accident. Pictured is the Boeing 737 that lost the forward upper half of its fuselage in-flight. Captain Robert Schornstheimer and First Officer Mimi Tompkins were able to maintain control of the aircraft and land it in Maui. One life was lost when a flight attendant was blown from the aircraft. May 1, 1988. (Dennis Oda)

Above: Hulihuli chicken. January 30,
1980. (Ken Sakamoto)

Above right: Waimanalo. 1980.
(Bob Young)

Right: Kaimuki Theatre. February 4, 1980.
(unknown)

Top left: James Grant Benton at his desk in the State Capitol. January 8, 1980. (Bob Young)

Top right: Frank De Lima. 1980. (Terry Luke)

Above left: Booga Booga, from left, Rap Reiplinger, James Grant Benton and Ed Ka'ahea . April 14, 1982. (Ken Sakamoto)

Above: Makaha Sons of Niihau, from left, Israel Kamakawiwoole, Mic Amina, and Skippy Kamakawiwoole. Front center is Moon Kawakahi. 1980. (Jerry Chong)

Mayor of Waimanalo

It took a while for Gabby Pahinui to earn the attention and acclaim that he deserved. He made his first recording in 1946, introducing the world to his mastery of kīhō'alu, or slack-key guitar, and he recorded steadily throughout the '50s and '60s, but it wasn't until the 1970s that he gained a wide audience. His albums from that later period cemented his reputation as a legend of the instrument and brought world musicians, like Ry Cooder, knocking on his door. However, it was Gabby's willingness to mentor young musicians, to give back to the community, that won him the respect of all who knew him. The weekend-long jam sessions held at his home in Waimanalo are the stuff of legend; many young musicians passed through his house on the way to greatness. He spent much time, in his later years, participating in State cultural programs, ensuring that Hawaiian music would continue to grow and be a part of the community from which it had sprung. Gabby died in 1980, but his timeless recordings continue to live on and inspire.

Top left: Gabby Pahinui at his Waimanalo home prior to the release of *The Gabby Pahinui Hawaiian Band, volume two*. February 24, 1977. (Ken Sakamoto)

Top right: Gabby Pahinui performing kiholau at an unknown location and event. 1975. (Bob Young)

Above: Last rites for slack-key musician and great Hawaiian singer Gabby Pahinui were held in the courtyard of Honolulu Hale. Pahinui was stricken with a heart attack and died on the Kahuku Golf Course. October 18, 1980. (Ken Sakamoto)

Left: A clan is born. From left to right: Pono and Louise Beamer, daughter Nona, her brother C. Keola, and Keola and Kapono. November 23, 1980. (Robert McCabe)

Below left: Don Ho pictured with his mother, Honey (left), and his wife, Melva. July 20, 1980. (Dennis Oda)

Above: Genoa Keawe at the Polynesian Society, Inc.'s luau for the Japanese CFC. November 8, 1981. (John Titchen)

Left: Eddie Kamae sings at a special Aloha United Way rally at the Fort Street Mall to draw attention to the fund drive. October 23, 1980. (John Titchen)

Right: Waikiki has become a shopping mecca, but a flood of new retail outlets means tougher competition for tourist dollars. The new Royal Hawaiian Center, right, has just opened and remains untried. The padlock on the door of Churchill's Inn symbolizes the fate of a number of Waikiki businesses. June 26, 1980. (Dennis Oda)

Below: Sunbathers work on their tans as they relax on the pier at Sans Souci Beach. October 7, 1980. (Ken Sakamoto)

Below right: Aerial of Waikiki, Ala Wai Golf Course, and Ala Wai Canal. November 17, 1980. (John Titchen)

Left: Construction on the Kaanapali Alii and the Marriott hotel is under way on Maui's "Gold Coast." August 10, 1980. (unknown)

Left: One of the few existing copies of Sheldon Dibble's History of the Sandwich Isles, printed at Hale Pa'i, Maui, in 1843. April 8, 1980. (Ken Sakamoto)

Above left: Linda Lingle. August 25, 1980. (unknown)

Above: Hannibal Tavares. November 12, 1981. (John Titchen)

Right: The staff of Tamashiro Fish Market in Kalihi are, from left to right, Guy Tamashiro, Walter Tamashiro, Larry Konishi, Johnny Tamashiro, and Cyrus Tamashiro. August 27, 1980. (Ken Sakamoto)

Below right: Lou Herman, a psychology professor who sometimes helps with the marine program at the University of Hawaii, measures a humpback calf as Kimo Mattoon, left, and Charlie Carr, right, assist. Mattoon and Carr are Punaluu residents who volunteered their help until the whale could be removed from shallow water. The man with the cap is Carry Chesswick from Sea Life Park. February 22, 1981. (Dean Sensui)

Left: Lehuanani Velasco directs eleventh grade singers at Kamehameha School. March 20, 1981. (Dennis Oda)

Below left: A somber part of the song for Kamehameha School's tenth grade boys. March 20, 1981. (Dennis Oda)

Below: Glen Grant, University of Hawaii lecturer, historian, and author of Obake Files. June 9, 1981. (Terry Luke)

Right: When the July heat sizzles out Haleiwa-way, there's one remedy island residents can rely on: shave ice. July 4, 1981. (Ken Sakamoto)

Below: Sid Fernandez. November 18, 1981. (Ken Sakamoto)

Below right: Ilikai Hotel, looking down Ala Moana Boulevard. February 8, 1982. (John Titchen)

Left: Jerry Santos after winning "Album of the Year." April 5, 1982. (Dennis Oda)

Below left: Bulldozers and cranes move around the vacant lot where the Alexander Young Building once dominated downtown Honolulu. September 14, 1981. (John Titchen)

Below: Former County Councilwoman JoAnn Yukimura attacked the County Planning Commission for retaining resort zoning for land near the controversial Nukolii project rather than changing it back to agriculture. December 16, 1981. (unknown)

Above right: Warehouse Area near the Schofield barracks where roofs were ripped off by Hurricane Iwa. November 29, 1982. (Ken Sakamoto)

Right: John Kelly, one of the founders of Save Our Surf. July 19, 1982. (Dennis Oda)

The Boy from Mauka Kona

Ellison Onizuka was a boy from Kona, a country kid. He was an Eagle Scout and a graduate of the University of Colorado at Boulder, earning a bachelor's degree in Aerospace Engineering. He was a test pilot for the United States Air Force and later an astronaut; he flew his first mission in January of 1985 on the Space Shuttle Discovery. He orbited the Earth for seventy-four hours. He was also a husband and the father of two girls. He was a man generous with his time, frequently returning to the Islands to speak with schoolchildren about his experiences, hoping to inspire them. When he boarded the Space Shuttle Challenger, he was our hero, and when he was lost on that unforgettable morning in 1986, something in us was lost, too. He'd done much to achieve his dreams, only to have his great effort wiped out in a single, awful instant. No, it is better to remember the man as he lived, as a boy from Kona, a country kid, who set his eyes on the stars and reached them.

Above: Astronaut Ellison Onizuka frequently visits classrooms statewide, encouraging children to pursue their ambitions. It is one of his ways of "giving back" to the isles. 1985. (unknown)

Top: A group of four- to seven-year-olds strum along at the Twelfth Annual Ukulele Festival at Kapiolani Park Bandstand. July 25, 1982. (Dennis Oda)

Above: Haunani Trask. August 15, 1986. (Terry Luke)

Space Shuttle Explodes; All 7 Aboard Are Killed

Tragedy Claims McAuliffe and Big Island's Onizuka

UH Regent Tells of Shock, Grief, Tears After Blast

Stunned President Reagan Defends NASA Safety Record

Top: Gone fishing. Anglers fish for halalu off Magic Island. March 22, 1983. (Ken Sakamoto)

Above: Wo Fat Chop Suey. July 6, 1983. (Terry Luke)

Right: Sunbathers pack the beach at Waikiki, a resort area that has just about reached its development capacity. Industry officials predict that tourism growth in the '80s will be on the Big Island and Maui. January 24, 1983. (unknown)

Top left: Representative Clayton Hee. February 2, 1983. (Terry Luke)

Top center: Joe Moore. February 10, 1983. (John Titchen)

Top right: Carole Kai. June 22, 1983. (Ken Sakamoto)

Above left: United Public Workers director Gary Rodrigues. February 8, 1984. (Ken Sakamoto)

Above center: Noriyuki "Pat" Morita: "I've been in and out of Hawaii for the last eighteen years. I'm a kotonk boy. Folks tell me I'm a favorite adopted kotonk." June 27, 1984. (Dean Sensui)

Above right: City Prosecutor Charles Marsland. April 25, 1985. (Dean Sensui)

Left: Retired wrestler Curtis Iaukea, known as "The Bull," is back in business—but as a manager this time. September 2, 1986. (Ken Sakamoto)

The Queen of Makaha

She was known as the Queen of Makaha. She loved the ocean—no surprise there, her middle name was Kapolioka'ehukai, "Heart of the Sea"—and had been surfing the waters around her home since small kid time. She began competing in surfing tournaments at the age of 14, often competing against and besting the boys around her because there were no separate heats for women. She was a fighter: she stood up for the rights of her fellow female wave-riders, helping to found the Women's Professional Surfing Association and the Women's Surfing Hui, and helping to organize the first all-female international surfing tour. At the age of 32, she was ranked the best in the world. Yes, she was a fighter and when she was diagnosed with breast cancer in 1983 she fought even harder. She raised awareness of the disease, helped to educate local women about breast cancer prevention, and still managed to find the time to surf every day. She held off the disease for 14 years, but it claimed her life on January 2, 1998. Thousands of people turned out for her memorial service. Her ashes were scattered in the waters off Makaha. The Queen of Makaha had returned to her home.

Above: Rell Sunn at Hang Ten women's surfing championship. December 17, 1979. (John Titchen)

Rell Sunn. May 23, 1983. (Dennis Oda)

Top: Masters finals consisted of, from left, Ben Aipa, John DeSoto, Paul Straugh, Alan Akuna, Drexel Wilson, and Leroy Achoy. June 12, 1983. (Dennis Oda)

Above: Surfing lesson. 1983. (unknown)

Above left: The waves were small, but the surfboards were plenty big at China's Longboard Surfing Contest in Waikiki. Showing off their longboards are, from left, Ann Chesser and her son Todd; and surfing legend Buffalo Keaulana and his son Brian. August 10, 1986. (Dennis Oda)

Right: Hon-Chew Hee in his studio with a watercolor scene of Kaneohe. August 10, 1983. (Terry Luke)

Below: Pegge Hopper in her studio with a painting of Lisa Au. "I was so angry about her murder, this was the only way I could deal with it." April 25, 1984. (Terry Luke)

Below right: The Natatorium provides a concrete frame for a tour boat off of Waikiki. September 1983. (Dean Sensui)

Left: Saleva'a Atisanoe. May 30, 1984. (John Titchen)

Below left: Jesse Kuhaulua receives a standing ovation before his final career bout against Masaduyama, whom he beat for a 4-4 record. June 3, 1984. (John Titchen)

Below: Honolulu businessman and *Star-Bulletin* chairman Chinn Ho finds himself surrounded by the winners of the Holoku Parade at the Forty-seventh Annual Holoku Ball. Pictured, from left, are U'ilani Baldwin, Emma Kim, Ho, Nalani Weeks, and Myrna Murdoch. June 8, 1984. (Dennis Oda)

Above: Brothers Cazimero. December 12, 1984. (Mike Tsukamoto)

Right: Merrie Monarch Festival. Pauoa Liko Ka Lehua Keolalaulani Halau Olapa O Laka. Kumu hula Aloha Dalire of Kaneohe. April 14, 1985. (Dennis Oda)

Below: Dancers from Halau Mohala Ilima in Kailua, Oahu, perform at the Merrie Monarch Festival under the guidance of kumu hula Mapuana de Silva. April 14, 1985. (Dennis Oda)

Top: Abigail Kekaulike Kawananakoa, daughter of Princess Piliuokalani Kawananakoa Morris, stands in front of Iolani Palace. June 7, 1985. (Dean Sensui)

Above: The Armed Services YMCA downtown is being put up for sale. August 2, 1984. (Terry Luke)

Right: Ronald Rewald, center, is accompanied by his wife, Nancy, and his attorney, Federal Public Defender Michael Levine, on the way to court for his trial on fraud charges. August 5, 1985.
(Terry Luke)

Above: Radio. Sandblaster-An Ala Moana beachgoer relaxes to the tunes of a nearby "boom box." Because of noise complaints, the city administration wants to tone down such devices at public parks and playgrounds. October 22, 1985.
(Craig T. Kojima)

Right: Mikela Keawe snags a cool drink as she and her pony trot by Kane's Kau Kau wagon on the North Shore near the Banzai Pipeline. March 26, 1985.
(Ken Sakamoto)

Above left: Vice President George Bush, accompanied by his wife, Barbara, chats with Pat Morita, center, and Ralph Macchio, stars of *Karate Kid II,* on the movie set in Kahaluu. October 11, 1985. (Ken Sakamoto)

Above: President Ronald Reagan and Nancy Reagan are shown strolling along Kahala Beach. April 1986. (Mike Tsukamoto)

Left: The United Jewish Appeal's Cavalcade of Stars fundraising dinner brings out a crowd of celebrities and politicians at the Kahala Hilton. They include the comedy team of Cheech and Chong, who flank Senator Daniel Inouye (center). December 2, 1985. (unknown)

Above: Hawaii Theater. 1986. (unknown)

Right: Coco Coffee House. July 16, 1986. (Dean Sensui)

Left: Tom Selleck playing volleyball. 1986. (Ken Sakamoto)

Below left: Charlene and Jack Thompson are dressed for business in the Tihati Productions office at the Moana Hotel. April 27, 1986. (Terry Luke)

Below: Comedians Frank De Lima and Mel Cabang. February 25, 1986. (Dennis Oda)

Top Right: Ferdinand Marcos's Niu Valley home. April 6, 1986. (Mike Tsukamoto)

Above: Former Philippine first couple Ferdinand and Imelda Marcos serenade supporters with "You Are The Only One I Am Going to Love" at the Blaisdell Center Arena. May 11, 1986. (Dennis Oda)

Right: The moon shines above the cross at the National Memorial Cemetery of the Pacific, Punchbowl, as people congregate for traditional Easter sunrise ceremonies. About 6,000 people attended. March 30, 1986. (Dennis Oda)

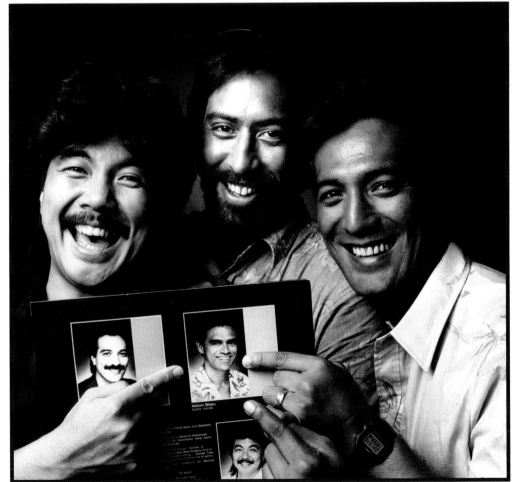

Above: Kaiser Hospital. October 1986.
(Craig T. Kojima)

Left: Kalapana are, from left to right,
Kenji Sano, D.J. Pratt, and Mackey Feary.
The three musicians point to the group's
missing fourth member, Malani Bilyeu.
September 23, 1986. (Dean Sensui)

Right: Patsy Mink greets John Waihee, one of her opponents in the Democratic primary for governor. At right is her husband, John Mink. September 22, 1986. (Ken Sakamoto)

Below right: John Waihee and his wife, Lynne, make their way to the bandstand at Iolani Palace, where Waihee would be sworn in as the fourth elected governor of Hawaii. December 1, 1986. (Ken Sakamoto)

BREATH TEST.

Top: Polynesian voyager Nainoa Thompson meets with more than four hundred Honganji Mission School students as they honor his accomplishment as navigator of the Hokulea. June 1987. (Craig T. Kojima)

Left: Hotel Lanai was built in the 1920s for guests of Dole Pineapple Company, which then owned ninety-eight percent of the island. May 6, 1987. (Mike Tsukamoto)

Above: Author A. Grove Day. February 12, 1987. (Dean Sensui)

Right: Chris and Patsy Hemmeter. 1989. (unknown)

Below right: Representative Neil Abercrombie, right, with Rene Mansho, left, and John Henry Felix after swearing-in ceremony. October 7, 1988. (Mike Tsukamoto)

Top: "The Fabulous Five," stars on the University of Hawaii's basketball team, are (from left) Al Davis, Bob Nash, Dwight Holiday, John Penebacker, and Jerome Freeman. 1989. (unknown)

Above: USS *Missouri* at Pearl Harbor. April 24, 1989. (Dean Sensui)

Below: A home for sale on Nehoa Street in Makiki welcomes foreign investors despite the controversy over Japanese investment in Hawaiian real estate. May 3, 1988. (Mike Tsukamoto)

Right: Tokyo billionaire Genshiro Kawamoto denies driving up home prices in Hawaii during his 1987 buying spree and claims that sellers who demanded high prices are responsible. In his first public appearance, at the Honolulu Press Club, Kawamoto said that he bought more than 170 apartments and single-family properties because he wanted to "contribute to Hawaii and be appreciated by the people." July 18, 1989. (Craig T. Kojima)

Right: Kamehameha Day Parade. June 10, 1989. (Ken Sakamoto)

Above: Michael Lucas, of Molokai Ranch sheep operations. The dog's name is Chief. August 3, 1989. (Mike Tsukamoto)

Left: Kapono Beamer and his mother, Winona Beamer. August 1, 1989. (Ken Sakamoto)

CHAPTER FOUR

1990
1999

Onipaʻa draws thousands 🐦 New Rainbow Warrior mascot 🐦 President Clinton plays golf 🐦 Helena's Hawaiian Food 🐦 June Jones comes to town 🐦 The last crop 🐦 Preparing andagi 🐦 Inside Harry's Music 🐦 *Baywatch* protects our beaches 🐦 Narcissus Queen hopefuls 🐦 Rural Hawaiʻi 🐦 Crack seed jars 🐦 Pets at Kalaupapa 🐦 Hawaiʻi's governors and mayors 🐦 A big imposing line 🐦 Kealiʻi Reichel's Hokus

Opposite page: Full solar eclipse from the top of Mauna Kea on the Big Island of Hawaii. In the foreground is the United Kingdom Infrared Telescope facility. July 11, 1991. (Dean Sensui) Above: Four generations: Brittany Lauren, six, hugs her mother, Rhonda Brown, thirty-two, while Rhonda's mother, Roberta Sunahara, fifty-five, stands next to her mother, Sumiko Kato, eighty-one. November 26, 1996. (Dennis Oda)

Above: Sumo wrestler Jesse Kuhaulua is greeted by Governor Waihee after a group photograph. February 15, 1990. (Dean Sensui)

Above right: Merrie Monarch Festival. A dancer from Keolalaulani Hula Olapa O Laka Leimomi Ho. Honolulu, Oahu. During Hula Auana. 1990. (Dennis Oda)

Right: Louisa Kamahalohanuilai and sons Iwi, four, Kami, three, Maleko, two, and Keoni, eight months, like their new home. May 16, 1990. (Craig T. Kojima)

Top: This aging house on Renton Road in Ewa Beach is considered noteworthy for the arched detailing under its eaves. July 12, 1990. (Craig T. Kojima)

Above left: Gustav Hannemann, left, chats with his son, Mufi, a Democratic candidate for the Second Congressional District, at Paradise Cove. August 16, 1990. (Dennis Oda)

Above: Glen Grant, University of Hawaii lecturer, historian, and author of Obake Files, is seen here with Gail Wozinea during a walking tour. August 31, 1990. (Terry Luke)

Right: The University of Hawaii introduces its new mascot — the Rainbow Warrior — during a football game against Texas A&M. September 1, 1990. (Ken Sakamoto)

Below: Citizens form a line to load bags of garbage onto a marine helicopter on Kahoolawe. October 18, 1990. (Craig T. Kojima)

Below right: Hanai Lhote, of Switzerland, hauls away discarded fishing nets and flotsam from Kanapou Bay on Kahoolawe. He was one of dozens of volunteers who collected debris to be hauled away by marine helicopters to a landfill. October 18, 1990. (Craig T. Kojima)

Left: In front of the Hilton Hawaiian Village in Waikiki, President George Bush swims with his shoes on. Afraid he might step on sharp coral, the Secret Service wanted the president to wear his jogging shoes in the ocean. October 28, 1990. (Dennis Oda)

Above left: At Hickam Air Force Base, President George Bush waves to a crowd estimated at five thousand people before boarding Air Force One back to Washington, D.C. October 29, 1990. (Dennis Oda)

Right: Iolani Palace curator Jim Bartels, left, carries the two royal crowns while Elia Long, a member of the palace board of directors, carries the scepter and sword of King Kalakaua and Queen Kapiolani in ceremonies at Iolani Palace. The crowns, made in London in 1882, were used in the coronation of the king and queen. November 16, 1990. (Dean Sensui)

Below right: Marines check motorists at Kaneohe Marine Base. The start of war with Iraq has resulted in stiffer security measures at state airports and military bases. January 16, 1991. (Craig T. Kojima)

Top: Narcissus Queen hopefuls at annual Narcissus Festival. Pictured in front (left to right): Rachelle Kauai Fa Ching, Monique Sai Mui Kan, Claire Suk Leng Lee, Erica Mai Liang Chang, Willow Lau Sinn Chang, and Anne Mai Li Co. In back, from left to right: Yan Yan Lau, Andrea Georgiana Chin An Yip, Vivian Wai Funn Chow, Sandra Yuk Lan Chan, Sharyn Noel Jung, Liang Ni, Heather Mai Hsinag Tsau, and Tracy Mew Lin Yuen. 1992. (Dennis Oda)

Left: Isaac Keao tenderly embraces his cat "Feisty." Since children are banned from Kalaupapa, a former leprosy settlement, pets are a welcome, common surrogate. April 13, 1992. (Dennis Oda)

Above: Richard Pupule, left, and National Park Service employee Albert Dudoit, center, help Teddy Gaspar celebrate his sixty-third birthday at Rea's Bar in the former leprosy settlement of Kalaupapa, Molokai. Mixing of residents and workers was unheard of in the years before leprosy medication existed. April 13, 1992. (Dennis Oda)

Top: A torchlight procession marches into Iolani Palace grounds for the centennial celebration of the Hawaiian monarchy. January 17, 1993. (Dennis Oda)

Right: Thousands flock to Iolani Palace in Honolulu, Hawaii, to show their support for the Hawaiian sovereignty movement. January 17, 1993. (Dennis Oda)

Left: Rick Gruzinsky inspects his shark-bitten surfboard. October 22, 1992. (Dean Sensui)

Below: Annette Miyashiro displays andagi, or Okinawan doughnuts, while behind her a crew busily turns out more and fries 'em up. The preparation of andagi and other Okinawan specialties was demonstrated at the Kariyushi VI festival at Hawaii Okinawa Center. May 22, 1994. (Ken Ige)

Left: Mahalo Airline. October 5, 1994. (Kathryn Bender)

Right: A hiker enjoys the mauka view from the Diamond Head Crater summit. Palolo Valley and Wilhemina Rise can be seen at the top left. March 17, 1995. (Dennis Oda)

Below: Trella Costa, from the ESPN TV show Bodies in Motion, on Kuhio Beach, Waikiki. April 19, 1995. (Ken Sakamoto)

Below right: Keiko Price, one of Hawaii's top swimmers. June 19, 1995. (Dennis Oda)

Above left: Keala Kennelly, Megan Abubo, and Rochelle Ballard are professional surfers. "We got swimsuit sponsors!" they shared after asking me to take their photo. November 13, 1995. (Ken Ige)

Top: Bishop Estate Trustees Lokelani Lindsey, Henry Peters, Richard Wong, Oswald Stender, and Gerard Jervis pose for photos at a dinner rally after a meeting over the lease-to-fee conversion process. May 24, 1995. (Dennis Oda)

Above: Kent Nakamura's family has been farming leased land in Kula for forty years, but Nakamura is planting his last crop. The land is to be broken up into two-acre lots and sold. "You can't stop it, right?" he says. "The agricultural community is getting smaller and smaller, so our power is getting smaller." October 13, 1995. (Gary T. Kubota)

Top: Shu Iwamoto, left, Roy Nakamura, center, and Wayne Miyashiro check their ulua poles at Kaena Point. October 20, 1995. (Dennis Oda)

Right: Richard Pua casts a fishing net in Hana Bay. December 12, 1995. (Ken Sakamoto)

Top: "Fore!" A golf ball sails over Kaena Point Satellite Tracking Station. November 29, 1995. (Ken Sakamoto)

Left: Aloha Tower Marketplace after sunset. November 16, 1995. (Dennis Oda)

Above: Roots and Wings. Fourth graders from James Todd's class at Ahuimanu Elementary perform at Hoomaluhia Botanical Garden. May 24, 1996. (Ken Ige)

Right: The Expression Session. Big surf at Waimea Bay. December 29, 1995. (Ken Sakamoto)

Below: A race official is flanked by a sea of green caps as 1,500 competitors from sixty countries prepare to start the grueling Gatorade Ironman Triathlon. 1996. (unknown)

Below right: At Ehukai Beach, signs warn people to stay out of the water because of strong currents. January 30, 1996. (Ken Sakamoto)

Local Grinds make good

Hawai'i may be the crossroads of the world geographically and geopolitically speaking, but for foodies, it is a culinary crossroads where the tastes of Asia and the Pacific meet those of Oceania and the Americas. Locals, of course, know that Hawai'i cuisine is the best in the world—whether it's grandma's kimchee, uncle's fried rice, or a superbly greasy spam musubi bought for a dollar at a convenience store, But it took a generation of local chefs to put the tastes of Hawai'i on the map. Chefs like Roy Yamaguchi, Sam Choy, and Alan Wong, to name a few, have brought local food to the world via their numerous cookbooks, restaurants, and television appearances. Now folks worldwide can sample the 'ono grinds we've been enjoying for years. Still, it's hard to believe that anyone on the mainland could equal the absolute sublimity of auntie's lomilomi salmon. But nice try, ne?

Above: Roy Yamaguchi. 1990. (Craig Kojima)

Top: Haleiwa. Chun's Market. 1996.
(Ken Ige)

Above: Eight-year-old Reese Suzuki executes a perfect "walk the dog" at the Oahu Island Yo-Yo Finals at Ala Moana Center. 1996. (George F. Lee)

Right: Hawaii's governor and mayors have their quarterly meeting at the Mauna Lani Resort. From left to right are Steven Yamashiro (Big Island), Mary Ann Kusaka (Kauai), Governor Cayetano, Jeremy Harris (Honolulu) and Linda Lingle (Maui). January 8, 1996. (Dennis Oda)

Below: *Crystal Symphony,* a cruise ship docked in Honolulu Harbor, appears to be turning up Bethel Street in downtown Honolulu. January 23, 1996. (Craig T. Kojima)

Below right: John Nahale Miranda holds a sawed-off shotgun to the head of hostage Tom McNeil outside a Honolulu waterproofing company where Miranda had recently been laid off. Miranda taped his right hand to the trigger and the gun barrel to McNeil's neck. The standoff ended several hours later when McNeil spun away from his captor and police shot and killed Miranda. February 6, 1996. (Ken Sakamoto)

Above left: Inside Harry's Music. Harry Yoshioka, Founder, and Clayton Yoshioka, President. March 19, 1996. (Ken Sakamoto)

Left: Crack seed jars at the Crack Seed Store on Koko Head Avenue, Kaimuki. April 10, 1996. (Ken Sakamoto)

Above: Bike Shop Stage Race. On the second and final lap of the Senior Women's Race, the peloton blazes down Kaukonahua Road toward Waialua at over forty-five miles per hour. May 19, 1996. (Dean Sensui)

Above right: Hawaiian recording artist Keali'i Reichel holds the five Hokus his album won. May 15, 1996. (Dennis Oda)

Right: Some of HFD's 77th recruit class take their oath of office. May 22,1996. (Dennis Oda)

Left: Irmgard Aluli at home with her guitar. July 15, 1996. (Craig T. Kojima)

Below left: Waianae divers (left to right) James Watanabe, Clinton Mendoza, Alfred Treu, Joe Tavita (right front), and Kahele Anderson (back right, in shirt) at Makua Beach. May 31, 1996. (Ken Ige)

Below: The men of Kealakapawa, led by kumu hula Michael Ka'ilipunohu Canopin, at the Twenty-third Annual King Kamehameha Hula Competition. June 21, 1996. (Dennis Oda)

Over the Rainbow

It is a song as familiar to local residents as the sound of birdsong in the morning or the lap of waves on a beach;, it begins with a husky voice saying, "'Kay, this one's for Gabby," and then the faint strumming of a ukulele comes in, followed by a haunting falsetto. It's Braddah Iz, of course, singing what would become his signature song, "Over The Rainbow/What A Wonderful World." It is that song that captures so many of the reasons why we loved Iz:, the laid back strumming of his uke, the voice, and his ability to project so much hopefulness. He began his career with the Makaha Sons during the Hawaiian Renaissance, and the group's song "Hawai'i '78" became an anthem of the movement. When he went solo in the early 1990s, his fame grew with the release of the classic album, *Facing Future*. His music was not limited to the islands; it began to appear in commercials, television programs, and films. Suddenly the man's music belonged to the world. But the man himself was always identified with the state he called home. When he passed away in 1997, we all felt the loss.

Above right: Israel Kamakawiwoole performs at the Na Hoku Hanohano Awards. May 15, 1996. (Dennis Oda)

Right: Thousands of mourners wait to pay their respects to the late Israel Kamakawiwo'ole as he lies in state at the Capitol building. July 9, 1997. (Dennis Oda)

Above: Assistant Instructor Charles Goodin, front, helps lead the Aiea Matsubayashi Ryu Karate Dojo. His sensei, William H. Rabacal (Sixth Dan Renshi), supervises on the left. July 13, 1996. (Dennis Oda)

Left: Kumu hula Joan Lindsey with her students. Pictured counterclockwise from the left are Staci Ihori, six, Dori Ann Saiki, seven, Kanani Numata, seven, Alana Park, seven, Megan Skinner, seven, Leina'ala Keohuloa, nine, Max Lindsey, eight, and Shannon Gibu, eight. July 23, 1996. (Dennis Oda)

Below: Kahuku watermelon farmers Ricardo Rabago (front left, holding melon), Clyde Fukuyama (back), and Mel Matsuda (right) with the season's first harvest. July 19, 1996. (Ken Ige)

WATERING THE LAWN IN MAKAKILO ...

Above: Farrington Prep football players form a big, imposing O-line. August 1996. (Ken Ige)

Above right: Keith Kekoa, eleven, a running back and linebacker for the Kaimuki Eagles football team, cools off at a water fountain during practice at Kilauea District Park. August 23, 1996. (George F. Lee)

Right: A south swell churns up good waves at the Kuhio Groin in Waikiki. July 23, 1996. (Dennis Oda)

Left: Kamehameha Garment Company at the Tenth Annual Governor's Fashion Awards. September 16, 1996. (Kathryn Bender)

Below left: Preparing food for an open house party on Tenth Avenue. In front, from left to right, are Fredo Pascua, Manny Hermano, and George Delaguiar. In back are neighbors Mickey Mitsunaga (left) and Clarence Tsuji. September 20, 1996. (Dennis Oda)

Below: George Kon, left, and Brad Fleener talk about Fleener's wildly painted car. Fleener, who rents part of Kon's home in Palolo Valley, spray-painted it himself. September 20, 1996. (Dennis Oda)

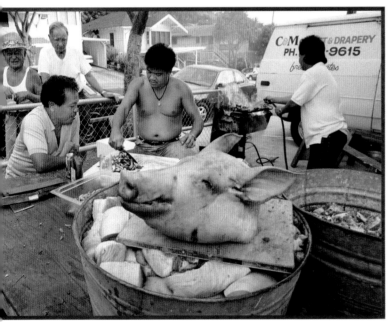

Above: Mana Manfredi (front), Christopher Amero (back), and Gregory Amero (right) lie in wait for tilapia during the "Catch and Release" fishing program at Hoomaluhia Botanical Gardens. October 6, 1996. (George F. Lee)

Above right: Leahi Frias, ten, looks in at neighborhood friend Derek Nuuihiwa's hula practice. She often comes to watch and practice on the sidewalk. September 24, 1996. (Dennis Oda)

Right: From left: Siblings Jason Miller, eleven, Jasmine Miller, twelve, and Jasha "J-Boy" Miller, eight, and brothers Johnathan Solomon, twelve, and James Solomon, twelve, have fun against a mural at the Palolo Valley Housing Center. September 23, 1996. (Dennis Oda)

Above left: First Hawaiian Tower. Honolulu's tallest building. October 16, 1996. (Ken Ige)

Left: Yashuko Doi Tanaka (bottom left) and Shigeo Matsumoto (bottom right) are original members of the Moiliili Hongwanji Mission. They are on hand to celebrate the Mission's ninetieth anniversary in Honolulu. October 20, 1996. (George F. Lee)

Above: Doug Beter has birds on his mind. Pictured is one of the show pigeons he releases at different ceremonies. After releasing his show pigeons he often offers children like these a close-up look at them. September 26, 1996. (Dennis Oda)

Above right: Malia Jones is a surfer, model, and entrepreneur. April 11, 1996. (Kathryn Bender)

Right: Women paddlers from the Outrigger Canoe Club are expected to place among the medal-winners at the Na Wahine O Ke Kai canoe race from Molokai. September 24, 1996. (Kathryn Bender)

Above Left: Mark Foo attends the Eddie Aikau Big Wave Service. November 6, 1996. (Craig T. Kojima)

Left: The Lanikai Canoe Club paddles into Waikiki Bay on its way to victory in the Molokai to Oahu Canoe Race. October 13, 1996. (George F. Lee)

Right: Helena Chock, center, has run Helena's Hawaiian Food for fifty years. These days she puts in a reduced eight-hour day and gets help from her grandson, Craig Katsuyoshi, left, and Ipolani Shiroma, right. November 14, 1996. (Ken Ige)

Above: A car hurries past a treacherous segment of Kamehameha Highway in Punaluu, where high waves surged across the roadway. The highway was strewn with rocks and sand, leading Oahu Civil Defense officials to urge caution while driving, particularly at night. November 11, 1996. (Craig I. Kojima)

Above right: Kristian Hegwood, a '96 graduate from Waianae High, undergoes the pressure of auditioning for a role in Miss Saigon. Among the judges are (left to right) Fred Hanson, Bob Billig, Peter Lawrence, Vinnie Liff, and Marc Oka. Hegwood, who never had voice lessons, earned a callback for a dance part. October 18, 1996. (Dennis Oda)

Left: Alana Dung sits in her Dad's lap after returning from Seattle where she received a bone marrow transplant. Parents Adelia and Stephen grin happily over their daughter's return and good health. November 14, 1996. (Kathryn Bender)

Left: President Bill Clinton makes a quick stop at the Waimanalo McDonald's following a round of golf at the Luana Hills Country Club in Kailua. November 16, 1996. (George F. Lee)

Above: Pearl Harbor survivors. From left are Donald Stratton, John Evans, Russell McCurdy, John Harris, Russell Lott, Joe Karb, Joe Langdell, Herbert Buehl, Clyde Combs, and Clinton Westbrook. December 4, 1996. (Ken Sakamoto)

Right: Brian Rivera, Reid Ginoza, and Ryan Nakatsuka, front row, play the ukulele. Manana Elementary program, Royal Shopping Center. December 17, 1996. (Craig T. Kojima)

Below: A scene from rural Hawaii: Sandy Cooper tends to her roadside fruit stand in Waikane. December 17, 1996. (Ken Sakamoto)

Below right: In observance of World AIDS Day, a candlelight vigil proceeds down Kalakaua to St. Augustine Church in Waikiki. Hawaii has the sixteenth-highest pearcentage of AIDS cases per capita in the nation. 190 countries participated. December 1, 1996. (Kathryn Bender)

Left: New first lady Vicky Cayetano shares a laugh with former first lady Jean Ariyoshi after Ariyoshi stepped back from fixing Cayetano's hair and fell over a footstool. May 6, 1997. (Dennis Oda)

Below: Watch your step! Anyone who has hiked or climbed knows that going down feels steeper than going up. Rain, of course, doesn't help. Tracy Masuda climbs the Haiku Stairs 1500 feet above the H3 freeway. May 13, 1997. (Ken Ige)

Above right: Darwin Rogers backs up against eventual sumo champion Craig Stevens in a match at Hawaiian Telephone. October 1, 1997. (Craig T. Kojima)

Right: 6'2" volleyball standout Lily Kahumoku (right side of net, center) is surrounded by her Kamehameha teammates. Lily wanted to include her teammates in this photo, preferring to keep the closeness of the group intact. October 2, 1997. (Dennis Oda)

Left: The Palolo Valley community has formed the Kalo Club in an effort to grow taro and other Hawaiian plants. October 5, 1997. (Kathryn Bender)

Below left: World champion tandem riders Bobby and Anna Shisler demonstrate their skills during "Expression Session" at the Makaha Oxbow Longboard Surfing Contest. October 28, 1997. (Craig T. Kojima)

Below: Four-year-olds at Moiliili Hongwanji Preschool say the pledge of allegiance to start the day. October 17, 1996. (Dennis Oda)

Above right: Men's halau at volcano.
April 15, 1998. (Dennis Oda)

Right: Linda Lingle campaigns for
supporters at the Dole Cannery Ballroom.
November 3, 1998. (Kathryn Bender)

Above: Vog shrouds Diamond Head at sunset as canoe paddlers make their way across Maunalua Bay in Hawaii Kai. Most of these paddlers are students at Kaiser and Kalani high schools. January 12, 1998. (Dennis Oda)

Left: Enjoying the sunset at Ala Moana Park are Ce Sargado, left, her friend Kealii Flood, and their dog "Liam." October 9, 1998. (Dennis Oda)

Below: Mike English with his wife, Desiree, and his two-year-old daughter, Victoria, at Ala Moana Beach. He put his daughter on his new surfboard and took her for a quick spin near shore before testing it out himself. December 20, 1998. (Dennis Oda)

Right: Newly appointed head football coach June Jones addresses the press in the dining room of Washington Place as Governor Ben Cayetano (center) and University of Hawaii Athletic Director Hugh Yoshida listen. December 14, 1998. (George F. Lee)

Below right: Charles Kane goes for "the big one" on his way to winning Sea Life Park's Belly Flop Contest. December 20, 1998. (George F. Lee)

Left: Sergeant Clayton Saito with his bike patrol on Hotel Street. In back are officers Hong Kim, Daniel Sellers, Apollo Chang, Kevin Lopez, and Tara Amuimuia. February 4, 1999. (Craig T. Kojima)

Below left: Anthrax threat at 1441 Ala Moana. Hazard materials team members going through a decontamination scrub down. February 23, 1999. (Ken Sakamoto)

Above: Nainoa Thompson and the Hokulea at sunset. April 24, 1999. (George F. Lee)

Above right: Inmates at Halawa Prison head off to lunch. The entire module goes at the same time, walking along "Main Street" in single file. April 15, 1999. (Dean Sensui)

Right: The Society of Seven take advantage of the swing revival to perform "Zoot Suit Riot" during the thirtieth anniversary show at the Outrigger Hotel. March 16, 1999. (George F. Lee)

Above: Palm tree grove on Niihau.
May 13, 1999. (Ken Sakamoto)

Left: Daniel Galera, left, and Ramonito
Flores ride on the back of a cone truck
on their way to cone off the contra-flow
lane of Kapiolani Blvd. May 21, 1999.
(Dean Sensui)

Right: Vietnam Veterans' Memorial Moving Wall. Patrick Patton of Stockton, California, makes a rubbing of his uncle's name, Enrique Soliz. May 21, 1999. (Ken Sakamoto)

Below right: Cloned male mouse, hanging, and donor. May 28, 1999. (Ken Sakamoto)

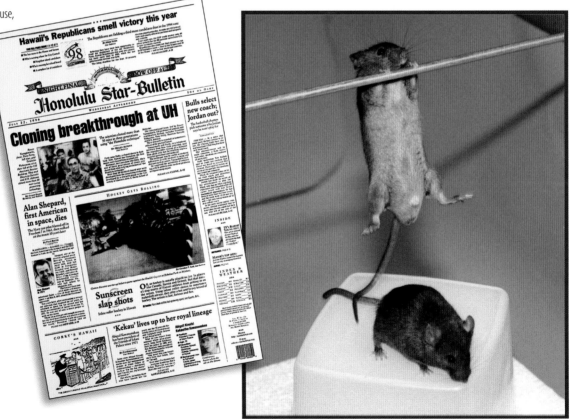

Left: Vernon Pai pulls into the parking lot of Andy's Drive-in with his 1934 Ford Three-Window Coupe. May 30, 1999. (George F. Lee)

Below left: Firefighter Jennifer Davis at Ewa Beach. June 18, 1999. (Craig T. Kojima)

"IN MASSACHUSETTS, DR. YANAGIMACHI CONFIRMED HIS EXPERIMENT BUT DECLINED TO REVEAL WHAT HE HAD CLONED..."

Right: Senior surfers, from left, Rabbit Kekai, Woody Brown, and John Kelly at Duke Kahanamoku Beach, Waikiki. June 28, 1999. (George F. Lee)

Below: Senior surfer Rabbit Kekai takes off on an offshore break, Waikiki Beach. June 28, 1999. (George F. Lee)

Below right: Rabbit Kekai at the Duke Kahanamoku statue in Waikiki. September 17, 1999. (Ken Ige)

Above: Faith and Mark Higashiguchi pose with their seven Shelties on a first-ever outing to Kapiolani Park. Next time, Faith says, they will bring the dogs in smaller groups. August 3, 1999. (Kathryn Bender)

Left: Doggie Cruuuuuuzin'. "Nikita" always rides back here, according to owner Michael Ward, who was on his way to work. July 9, 1999. (Ken Ige)

Above: Women in kimonos preparing to honor John A. Burns at Punchbowl. July 26, 1999. (Craig T. Kojima)

Right: (top to bottom) Kalai Pili-Peapealalo, nine, Bronston Pili-Peapealalo, eight, George Peapealalo, twelve, and Wayneson Tanouye, eleven, play in the waters of Kahana Valley. Jordan Peapealalo, eight, is on the far right. August 18, 1999. (Kathryn Bender)

Left: The first Paniolo Hall of Fame, initiated by the Oahu Cattlemen's Association, featured the five inductees at Honolulu Hale. From left to right: Dr. Max B. Smith, Albert Silva, Abraham Akau, George K. A'i Sr., and Ron Brun. August 24, 1999. (Kathryn Bender)

Below left: Sitting along Hotel Street in Chinatown. August 28, 1999. (Kathryn Bender)

Below: Master craftsman Jose Hipolito Jr. is retiring from the Kamaka Ukulele Factory where he has worked since 1955. Hipolito, who is deaf, tunes the ukulele by feeling the string's vibration on the wood. He is pictured here with Samuel Kamaka, owner of Kamaka Ukuleles. August 31, 1999. (Craig T. Kojima)

Right: David Hasselhoff gives Governor Cayetano a *Baywatch Hawaii* movie clapper prior to a group shot. September 1, 1999. (Dennis Oda)

Below: Three *Baywatch* extras walk through a scene as the cameras pan to David Hasselhoff on another part of the set. September 1, 1999. (Dennis Oda)

Below right: Aah, the good life. Jesse Spencer, who was attacked by a shark while surfing in Kona, gets a walk-on part in *Baywatch Hawaii*. Here he is with some of the stars. November 23, 1999. (Ken Ige)

Left: More than one thousand hula dancers from thirty halaus gather at Aloha Tower. September 19, 1999. (George F. Lee)

Above: Piilani Kalingo, of Hawaiian Building Maintenance, cleans windows overlooking 1132 Bishop Street. September 21, 1999. (Ken Ige)

Running, running, running

Every great city demands a great race—New York, Boston, Chicago, etc, all lend their names to premier marathons that course through their city streets each year. We got ours in 1973 when the first Honolulu Marathon was run. Local residents Duncan Macdonald and June Chun won the race in that inaugural year. (Macdonald would win it again in 1976.)Since then the list of participants and winners has become a multicultural who's who of the running world. Competitors from as far away as Kyrgystan race each year and the field continues to grow and grow, sometimes numbering upwards of 27,000 entrants. And with the possible exception of a few Hawaii Kai residents whose driveways get blocked for the route every second Sunday in December, everyone in town is happy to cheer on the racers passing by.

Above: Trying to avoid the rain before the start of the Honolulu Marathon, runners gather under a roofed gas island at a 7-11 store on Ala Moana and Queen Streets. December 12, 1999. (Dennis Oda)

Above: Paddlers glide down the Ala Wai Canal as a reflection of a Waikiki building juts across the water. November 17, 1999. (Ken Ige)

Left: The sun sets on the Puowaina Young Riders Pop Warner football team as they practice at Stevenson Intermediate School. October 27, 1999. (Dennis Oda)

Below left: Suspected Xerox gunman Byran Uyesugi is brought into the receiving desk of the Honolulu Police Department following a six-hour standoff in Honolulu Park. Seven Xerox employees were shot. November 2, 1999.
(George F. Lee)

CHAPTER FIVE

2000
2009

Marines return home ❦ Merrie Monarch kahiko ❦ WAC champions ❦ *American Idol*'s Jasmine Trias ❦ go!'s nineteen-dollar airfare ❦ Hawai'i Superferry debuts ❦ *Pearl Harbor* premiere ❦ Tadd Fujikawa qualifies for Sony ❦ Jack Johnson encore at Kōkua Festival ❦ Hawai'i Big Boys Show ❦ Aloha, Aloha Airlines ❦ Little League World Series champs ❦ Opening day polo ❦ A shower from Dad ❦ Cheerleading competition ❦ Catching 'ahi

Opposite page: Aunty Genoa Keawe performed at the Hawaiian Vote Concert and Rally. The organizers announced that they will continue their year-round mission to get more native Hawaiians registered to vote in future elections. November 4, 2006. (Dennis Oda) Above: Amateur Tadd Fujikawa celebrates after making an eagle putt on the 18th hole. He shot 66 to finish 3 under in the second round to make the cut at the 2007 Sony Open. He just turned 16, Jan. 8th and is the youngest player to make a PGA cut in 50 years. January 12, 2007. (Dennis oda)

Right: Vanna White talks with Chef Sam Choy at the Waialae Country Club. January 16, 2001. (Craig T. Kojima)

Below: Park-goer Jong Shin takes time to hand-feed the Java Rice Finches at Magic Island. January 10, 2001. (George F. Lee)

Below right: Chow Hop Ng, owner of Shung Chong Yuein, a Chinatown bakery, with a tray of Gao. Gao is a sweet pudding traditionally made in celebration of the Chinese New Year; it symbolizes keeping the family together. January 23, 2001. (Ken Sakamoto)

Above: With the lights of Waikiki in the background, Mark Heckman (center in a light t-shirt), Waikiki Aquarium Staff and Community Enrichment Programs Coordinator, explains to the group of reef walkers how to find reef-dwelling creatures. February 23, 2001. (Dennis Oda)

Left: Tau Dance Theater dancers rehearse for "Ladies Night Out" at Mid-Pacific Institute. From left, Cora Yamagata, Esther Izuo and Ann Smith. March 25, 2001. (F.L. Morris)

Above: Opening day of the 2001 polo season at the Waimanalo Polo Grounds. Mike Ebinger walks some of the "ladies" across the field. Polo ponies are predominantly mares (female). April 29, 2001. (F.L. Morris)

Right: Paia Mill is a closed sugar mill at Paia, Maui. May 3, 2001. (F.L. Morris)

Above: As the funeral procession for Dannygriggs Padayao goes by HPD headaquarters on Beretania Street, police officers line up and salute the passing cars. May 17, 2001. (Dennis Oda)

Left: A movie poster of Pearl Harbor looms large over the refreshment area of the makeshift movie theater built atop the flight deck of the USS *John C. Stennis* for the premiere of *Pearl Harbor*. May 21, 2001. (George F. Lee)

Below: From left, Dan Ackroyd, Tom Sizemore, Alec Baldwin, Cuba Gooding Jr., Kate Beckinsale and Josh Hartnett applaud as leading man Ben Affleck is introduced to the gathered audience on the USS *John C. Stennis*. May 21, 2001. (George F. Lee)

Above: These Moanalua High students (from left) Jeremy Kam, Kapono Haynes and Jon Bareng dug a pit in the sand and were buried in it by their friends at Sandy Beach. May 23, 2001. (Dennis Oda)

Right: At Barber's Point, for the movie-making of *The Ride,* the actors are all dressed in fashions from the early 1900s. Sean Kaawa, who plays Duke Kahanamoku in the movie, poses with his very heavy board. May 25, 2001. (Craig T. Kojima)

Above left: An old man takes his lunch inside the stoop of a Hotel Street store. June 5, 2001. (Craig T. Kojima)

Above: Shane Aquino tends a flock of barbequeing chicken at Stanley's BBQ Chicken stand on Auahi Street. The stand has been selling chicken every Saturday for the last four years. June 9, 2001. (Richard Walker)

Left: Lisa Matsumoto as Da Wicked Queen in *Once Upon One Kapakahi Time* at Hawaii Theatre. 2002. (Ken Ige)

Above: These Punahou girls were scheduled to participate in a paddling competition, but the races were canceled. They find a way of releasing race day tensions with a little play in the mud. January 29, 2002. (Don Kozono)

Above right: Baby Kamohaiki Krainer stands next to the heavily tattooed leg of his grandfather, Chief Miko. They were on-hand for the Ala Wai Challenge held at Ala Wai Park. January 20, 2002. (F.L. Morris)

Right: Kalani and Kaiser High School girls after they finished their outrigger canoe practice at Maunalua Bay. February 5, 2002. (Dennis Oda)

Above left: Local comic Frank De Lima spoofs the songs and singers of KOHO radio during his return engagement at the Palace in Waikiki. February 22, 2002. (George F. Lee)

Above: Jake Shimabukuro. March 4, 2002. (Craig T. Kojima)

Left: Dwayne "The Rock" Johnson, WWE wrestler and film star, gives a shaka to a friend during a press conference at the Blaisdell Galleria. June 13, 2002. (Richard Walker)

Right: Visitors and kamaaina alike enjoy the movies and food sponsored by the City and County at Waikiki Beach as a part of Sunset on the Beach. June 16, 2002. (George F. Lee)

Below: In the dressing room, Lynn Racoma, left, and Amy Hayashida prepare for the Hawaii Figure Contest at the Hawaiian Islands Bodybuilding Championships at the Blaisdell Concert Hall. Lynn finished in third place and Amy in second place to winner, Kristi Tauti. June 29, 2002. (Dennis Oda)

Below right: The top winners in their weight divisions in a "pose down" to determine the overall winner at the Hawaiian Islands Bodybuilding Championships. From left to right, Neilsen Murakami, Tarrell Giersch, Francis Taua, Nos Racoma and Chris Yelton. Tarrell, the heavyweight champion, then took the overall title. June 29, 2002. (Dennis Oda)

"NO LIGHTS. THIEVES GOT OUR COPPER WIRES."

Left: Pake Zane, a noted local collector inside his store, Antique Alley. His wife, Julie Lauster, is in her "office" on the left, surrounded by their inventory. July 26, 2002. (Dennis Oda)

Below left: Hula Halau 'O Kaleolani—under the direction of kumu hula Benjie Kaleolani Santiago—during the hula auana competition at the Twenty-seventh Annual Queen Lili'uokalani Keiki Hula Competition. July 27, 2002. (Dennis Oda)

Below: Amber Nathaniel competes in the girls ten-to-twelve solo dance competition at the Fifth Annual Iahiti Fete of Hawaii at Aloha Tower Marketplace. October 5, 2002. (Richard Walker)

Pageants for Everyone

There's no shortage of beauties to be found in the islands and there is no shortage of pageants to showcase those beauties. It would be a safe bet to assume that there is a beauty pageant for nearly every ethnicity in the Pacific Rim underway at any given moment somewhere in the state. For that matter, it would be safe to assume that there is pageant catering to every demographic, age group, and martial status underway as well. We love pageants here. We love watching the young ladies in their slinky dresses strut down the runway looking for a chance at grabbing the title of Miss Hawaii, or Miss Hawaii, USA, or Mrs. Hawaii, or Miss Narcissus Festival, or Cherry Blossom Queen, or Miss Hawaii-Filipina, or one of the myriad other variations on the theme. There's really no explaining our fascination with pageants, except—and this is hardly the most progressive of thoughts—it is often nice to look at a pretty woman.

Above: 9th Annual Western Union Filipino Fiesta & Parade from Ala Moana Beach park to Kapiolani Park. Filipino beauty Queen hopefuls including the reigning Miss Oahu Filipina, Sherilyn Baclig in pink and behind her, Miss Hawaii Filipina, Jennifer Bayudan. May 12, 2001. (Ken Sakamoto)

Top: Jumpers get one last splash as visitors and malahini alike crowd the pier at the Kapahulu Groin to see the sunset. June 2, 2003. (George F. Lee)

Above: Kaipo, a service dog belonging to Derek Salis, second from right, enjoys a longstanding summer activity as he gets buried in the sand at Ala Moana Beach Park. August 31, 2003. (George F. Lee)

Above left: Marlene Kamakawiwo'ole is all smiles as she stands next to a sculpture of her late husband, Israel Kamakawiwo'ole, that was unveiled during the dedication ceremony at the Waianae Neighborhood Community Center. September 20, 2003. (Dennis Oda)

Above: Vili Fehoko (UH Warrior) is pictured "in the jungle" in front of Bachman Hall at UH. The UH homecoming concert is scheduled to be on the lawn at Bachman Hall. Ho'onu'a with Christian Yrizarry and Jared Keo are headliners. October 21, 2003. (Dennis Oda)

Left: President George W. Bush gets lei and a hug from a Pearl Harbor Elementary School student during his read-aloud session. October 23, 2003. (George F. Lee)

Right: These chefs pose to promote a fund-raising event featuring Hawaiian food, especially taro. November 5, 2003. (Craig T. Kojima)

Below right: The lifeguards at Sandy Beach keep a close eye on the high surf. Sandy Beach was closed, and sightseers were kept on the far side of the beach-access road. November 21, 2003. (Dennis Oda)

Above: Saint Francis School Pacific Club members, from left, Elise Tima, Kanoe Vierra, and Alyssa Fernandez dance a hula during the Pro Bowl Football Festival and Appreciation Day at Kapiolani Park. February 7, 2004. (Ronen Zilberman)

Left: Nohealani Canon, left, and the rest of the dancers from Halau O'naleio'kamakani perform the hula during Brunch on the Beach in Waikiki. February 15, 2004. (Ronen Zilberman)

Above: The Byodo Temple in the Valley of the Temples off Kahekili Hwy. March 22, 2004. (Dennis Oda)

Right: From left are Marci Lobendahn, her brothers Joe and Willy, and Fred Salanoa. Marci, a Pearl City graduate, will attend Missouri Valley College to play volleyball and basketball. Joe, a junior linebacker at the University of Washington, and Willy, who will play football at Virginia Union University, are both St. Louis graduates. Fred Salanoa graduated from Radford High School and is now its head football coach. Here they share a laugh outside the Radford High School gym. June 22, 2004. (Dennis Oda)

Above: Aiea High School kids decided to visit Kakaako Park to hang out. They went to the top of the hill and jumped around, while one of them videotaped them. January 4, 2005. (Dennis Oda)

Left: Maryknoll High School senior Kori Mijo put together a Locks of Love drive that uses donated hair to provide hairpieces to financially disadvantaged children under eighteen with medical hair loss. This is Jessica Kaniho, an instructor at Honolulu Community College, measuring Harold Tarumoto's hair. January 8, 2005. (Dennis Oda)

Above right: Kaneohe-based marines take some time out to attend a memorial service at Kaneohe Marine Base Head-quarters for ten marines killed in Iraq. The honored dead include Lance Corporal Blake Magaoay from Pearl City. January 13, 2005. (Craig T. Kojima)

Right: On Chinese New Year, many people make lo-hei, a traditional salad that the diners toss in the air for good luck. From left to right, after tossing the salad, George Moniz (left), Allison Ramberg, Greg Wong, Tristan Choi, Gemma Brown, Brandie Kamiya, Michelle Agasa, Vivienne Gan, Sornkom Sangngam, and Naomi Kodama. January 31, 2005. (Craig T. Kojima)

Above left: Lucille, a golden retriever, sits on her nightly perch surveying the neighborhood and ocean view from her St. Louis Heights home. February 18, 2005. (Lucy Pemoni)

Above: Makana Kamanuwai, two, of Manoa has some big shoes to fill after swimming with her mother near Kewalo Basin. March 4, 2005. (Jamm Aquino)

Left: A homeless man sits at a bus stop on the corner of Ward Avenue and Kapiolani Boulevard. February 21, 2005. (F.L. Morris)

Above: Eleven-year-old Tae Keller, left, and her sister, Sunhi, five, are both blossoming poets, following in the footsteps of their mother, renowned author Nora Okja Keller. March 5, 2005. (Jamm Aquino)

Above right: Models pose in spring fashions inside Neiman Marcus at Ala Moana Shopping Center. Models are Ying Ying, left, and Cassandra Eaton. February 18, 2005. (F.L. Morris)

Right: Radford High School student Brittiany Broadwater and others during cheerleading practice in the school gym. March 7, 2005. (F.L. Morris)

Above left: David Illenado escorts Jeremi Guillermo, left, Ashley Madela, Haydee Tolentino, and April Pacpaco. All are seniors from Kapolei High. March 11, 2005. (Craig T. Kojima)

Left: Hoala School kids in Wahiawa color their Easter eggs. Left to right, in the front row, are Angel Bayot, Parker Hill, Aaron Norton, Zoie Bactista, Victoria Peters, Manya Tam and Brianne Kiaaina; left to right, in the back row, are Kai Poarch, Matthew Norton and Noah Ballaibe. March 18, 2005. (Dennis Oda)

Right: After Maile Emily Kau'ilaniona'opu-aehi'ipoiokeanuenueokeola Francisco is announced the winner of the Miss Aloha Hula competition at the Forty-second Annual Merrie Monarch Festival, (left to right) Jennifer Oyama (2003 Miss Aloha Hula winner), kumu hula Sonny Ching, Francisco, and Natasha Akau (2004 Miss Aloha Hula winner) are so emotional. March 31, 2005. (Dennis Oda)

Below: Eight-month-old Deanette Dino of Kalihi gets a shower from dad, Dino Matto, after swimming at Ala Moana Beach Park. March 29, 2005. (Craig T. Kojima)

Below right: Leonora Ching and her pickles. April 9, 2005. (Craig T. Kojima)

Above: For the finale of the Second Annual Kokua Festival, (left to right) John Cruz, Jackson Browne, and Jack Johnson appear on stage together. April 16, 2005. (Dennis Oda)

Left: The crowd goes wild at the Second Annual Kokua Festival, which features G. Love & Special Sauce, Osomatli, John Cruz, Jackson Browne and Jack Johnson. Proceeds go toward supporting the Kokua Hawaii Foundation, an environmental organization Johnson co-founded. April 16, 2005. (Dennis Oda)

Right: Kamehameha School's Kamehameha Dance Company presents "Balance," a contemporary dance performance in the Princess Ruth Keelikolani Auditorium. The performance is a benefit for Prevent Child Abuse Hawaii. Kalei Auld performs with other dancers. May 8, 2005. (F.L. Morris)

Above: The Baby Crawling Contest (presented by Jamba Juice) provides excitement for the whole family at the Eighth Annual New Baby Expo 2005 held at the Blaisdell Exhibition Hall. At the start of the heat, the adults all try to get their child to crawl across the mat. May 21, 2005. (Dennis Oda)

Right: Kamamalahoe Canoe Club practice in Keehi Lagoon. Chanelle Koja-Cristobal (front), Chris Schoknecht (behind Chanelle), and other paddlers from the club start their workout. July 15, 2005. (Dennis Oda)

Above left: Jasmine Trias takes a break from lunch at Palomino's to pose with her new CD. July 7, 2005. (Dennis Oda)

Left: Bar 35 at 35 Hotel Street has at least one hundred different types of beer. Libette Garcia (left) and George Seabolt (right) hold some of the different types of beers served. July 16, 2005. (Dennis Oda)

Above right: The eighth annual harmonica recital presented by the Hawaii Harmonica Society in Mission Memorial Auditorium. From left to right, Seiko Imoto, Take Tanigawa, Florence Hagino and Lenette Tam along with other members of the Small World Harmonica Band play on stage. August 7, 2005. (F.L. Morris)

Right: Alakai Aglipay (left), Vonn Fe'ao, and Zachary Rosete stand at the center of attention in a crowd of Ilima School classmates. The whole school is out cheering and honoring the 2005 Little League World Series champs. September 8, 2005. (Craig T. Kojima)

Left: The pond on the ewa end of Ala Moana Park is lined with birds. They take flight and follow this man as he dumps about thirty-five pounds of birdseed. October 21, 2005. (Dennis Oda)

Below left: PBS (Public Broadcasting Service) Hawaii is celebrating its fortieth anniversary. Mike McCartney, PBS Hawaii President and CEO, poses for a picture with some of the favorite characters. November 4, 2005. (Dennis Oda)

Below: The Dog, also known as Duane Lee Chapman, and Beth Barmore joke around as they walk down Queen Emma Street. November 11, 2005. (Cindy Ellen Russell)

Above: Volleyball players at Fort DeRussy are silhouetted against the Waikiki shores during the late afternoon. December 9, 2005. (Cindy Ellen Russell)

Right: From left, Jonathan Butac, Romel Ventura, and Anthony Deguzman jump as their friend, Kevin Kumoto (not shown), takes their picture at Ala Moana Beach during sunset. November 15, 2005. (Dennis Oda)

Left: Briana Solidum is the administrative assistant for Washington Place. Solidum works in the Office of the Governor for events related to the historic landmark and helps arrange public tours of the property. November 16, 2005. (Cindy Ellen Russell)

Below left: Mayor Mufi Hannemann in Honolulu Hale. December 21, 2005. (unknown)

Right: Don Freitas, left, and his crewman, Daniel Silva, hold up four ahi they caught. Each ahi weighs 150 to two hundred pounds, enough to feed their family and friends. December 29, 2005. (unknown)

Below: Shayani Dudoit-Gamit, five years old, lives in Kaunakakai, Molokai. November 21, 2005. (Craig T. Kojima)

Below right: Hawaiian musician and Grammy-nominee Raiatea Helm at the Hawaii State Art Museum during Live on the Lawn concert. January 6, 2006. (Richard Walker)

Above left: Women of Ahahui Kaahu-manu sit in the entrance to Iolani Palace during a ceremony commemorating the 113th anniversary of the overthrow of the Hawaiian Monarchy. January 15, 2006. (Richard Walker)

Above: Aleia Monden, from St. Andrew's Priory, is the defending three-time girls diving champion in the state, a two-time high school All-American, and the current AAU champion. Here, she is participating in an ILH diving meet at Punahou High School pool, which she won. January 28, 2006. (Dennis Oda)

Left: A rainy day is not enough to keep boogie-boarders Christian Awaya, left, and Keoni Manago from having a great time on a flooded Manoa field. January 25, 2006. (Craig T. Kojima)

Above: The third and final round of the Fields Open at Ko Olina. Michelle Wie reacts after making a long birdie putt. She finished third at thirteen under, as Meena Lee beat Seon Hwa Lee in a play-off to win. February 25, 2006. (Dennis Oda)

Right: The Bowman family takes in the scenery at Waimanalo Bay as their golden lab, Gordon, peers behind. February 15, 2006. (Cindy Ellen Russell)

Left: Halau Hula Olana under the direction of kumu hula Howard Ai and Olana Ai dance during the auana portion of the Merrie Monarch Festival hula competition. April 13, 2006. (Dennis Oda)

Below: Ka Leo O Laka I Ka Hikina O Ka La (kane) under the direction of kumu hula Kaleo Trinidad dance during the auana portion of the Merrie Monarch Festival hula competition. Trinidad's halau took second in both kahiko and auana and second overall in kane. April 13, 2006. (Dennis Oda)

A Legacy of Tradition

For nearly 50 years, folks have been crowding Hilo every spring for the biggest event in competitive hula—the Merrie Monarch Festival. Established to honor the memory of King David Kalākaua—the titular monarch—who helped revive ancient cultural traditions that had been all but eradicated following the arrival of the missionaries in the 18th and 19th centuries, the festival has, in the intervening years, taken on a bit of showbiz glamour as halaus strut their stuff in dazzling, sometimes revealing, outfits. But outfits and glitz aside, what the crowds come for, and what viewers at home watch for, is the dancing, the hula. There is something about watching a dancer moving so fluidly on that stage that is somehow otherworldly. So we watch and are captivated and pick our favorites and cheer on the winners, and when it's all over we'll feel that tiny bit of regret that comes from knowing we've got to wait an entire year to get to experience it all over again.

Above: Leilani Rojas during the auana portion of the Miss Aloha Hula competition at the Merrie Monarch Festival. She belongs to Halau Keali'i O Nalani under the direction of kumu hula Keali'i Ceballos. April 12, 2007. (Dennis Oda)

Right: Jeana Inouye leaps through the air during the dance performance "Chanson Joie de Vivre" at the Hawaii Theatre. The dance is part of Mid-Pacific School's Pupukahi i ke alo o na pua Spring Concert *Pikorua*. May 7, 2006. (Cindy Ellen Russell)

Below: *The Star of Honolulu* pulls into Aloha Tower Marketplace after a sunset cruise. May 20, 2006. (Cindy Ellen Russell)

Above: Richard Silvius practices his sax at Ala Moana Beach Park. He says he usually goes there everyday to practice, so he doesn't bother his neighbors. June 1, 2006. (Dennis Oda)

Left: *MidWeek* publisher Ron Nagasawa, seated front, at the Ocean Club. May 27, 2006. (John Berger)

Above: Takejiro Higa, eighty-three, in his Kalihi home. The World War II veteran is one of eighty-six Japanese-American veterans who will be honored by the Okinawan government for their role in saving lives of Okinawan citizens. June 2, 2006. (Cindy Ellen Russell)

Right: Go's CRJ-200. The new inter-island carrier will begin flying customers and announced $19 one-way fares for a limited time as a promotion. June 7, 2006. (Cindy Ellen Russell)

Above: Florence Marton holds up two issues of the National Inquirer in which she was featured with some of her estimated 10,000 Barbie dolls. Following a heart attack she has not been able to maintain her collection, which she keeps in her extended garage. She hopes to auction it off as one collection to someone in Hawaii. June 17, 2006. (Dennis Oda)

Left: Hawaiian monk seal R5AY on the North Shore with her new pup. While pups have been born on Rabbit Island in recent years, this is the first monk seal born in a public area on Oahu since 1998. NOAA Fisheries Service and Oahu Hawaiian Monk Seal Response Team staff and volunteers monitor the site. June 9, 2006. (Dennis Oda)

Right: An unidentified girl surfer cuts back on a late afternoon wave at Kewalo's surf break at the entrance to Kewalo Basin. June 17, 2006. (F.L. Morris)

Below right: The Twenty-ninth Prince Lot Hula Festival was held at Moanalua Gardens. These Japanese tourists (left to right) Ryoka Gobuki, Shinko Matsunaga, and Kumiko Tominaga enjoy going over their pictures on their digital camera. July 8, 2006. (Dennis Oda)

Left: A skateboarder cruises the slopes of the skate park at Keolu Playground. July 19, 2006. (Cindy Ellen Russell)

Below left: While playing wheelchair tennis at the Ala Moana Park tennis courts, Rich Julian practices his returns. July 25, 2006. (F.L. Morris)

Above right: University of Hawaii senior defensive back Leonard Peters is a competitive fireknife dancer when not playing football. July 27, 2006. (Jamm Aquino)

Right: Brother Noland jams with saxophonist Fred Li during KCCN's Sixteenth Birthday Bash at the Waikiki Shell. July 29, 2006. (Jamm Aquino)

Top: Melveen Leed, front center in a white dress, and her husband, Al Dacascos, to Melveen's left, moments after their wedding. August 19, 2006. (John Berger)

Above: From left, Vail, 27 (son of Hubert), Hubert, 51 (son of Herbert) and brothers Albert, 81, Gilbert, 91 and Herbert Minn, 83, pose for a group picture at Herbert's Manoa home. August 11, 2006. (Dennis Oda)

Above: Maili Beach residents Dino Palisbo and girlfriend Christie Kealoha do not know where their next move will take them. Residents of Maili Beach Park, as well as other beach parks along Oahu's leeward coast, are alarmed; some have nowhere to relocate to. August 27, 2006. (Jamm Aquino)

Above right: Rihanna and Tom Moffatt at Pipeline Cafe. September 15, 2006. (John Berger)

Right: From left, Topher Erickson, Justin Rice, Jeanne Rice, and Alan Rice make their way past the point at Magic Island at dusk. Segways are becoming very popular on the streets of Honolulu. August 11, 2006. (Jamm Aquino)

Above: Trump sales event in the Halekulani hotel ballroom. The crowd is made up of prospective buyers of units at the planned Trump Waikiki tower. October 9, 2006. (F.L. Morris)

Left: The Waikiki Beach Walk project under construction. October 30, 2006. (George F. Lee)

Local Boy Makes Good

Barack Obama has fast become Hawaii's favorite son. Anyone watching the television news coverage of the charismatic Senator is familiar with his story: Born to a white mother and black father, Barack Obama in Honolulu, his parents divorced and he bounced around in Indonesia for a few years with his mother and step-father before returning to Hawai'i to live with his grandparents. He attended Punahou School—his friends knew him as Barry—and once he graduated, he moved on to a distinguished academic career eventually earning a law degree from Harvard. His ascendancy in politics has been meteoric—beginning with a seat in the Illinois State Senate, then moving on to the U.S. Senate, and now a presidential candidate. It isn't difficult to see why we here in Hawai'i love Barack so much. He represents so much of what makes this state great, but what is often ignored by outsiders. He's a product of a Hawai'i school and a Hawai'i upbringing, and like many of us here, he comes from a multi-ethnic background. He's proving to our country and the world just what a person from Hawai'i is capable of.

Above: Illinois Senator elect, Barack Obama, spoke at a press conference prior to the Democratic Party fundraiser in the Hilton Hawaiian Village. December 16, 2004. (FL Morris)

Top: Asia Leong's jewelry has attracted clientele such as Madonna and Lauren Hill. Leong is currently based in Paris and Kauai. November 5, 2006. (Cindy Ellen Russell)

Above: Sometimes the only way to bring game out of the bush is to carry it, as Erland Pahukoa (middle) demonstrates after a pig hunt in the Kipahulu area of east Maui. Pictured with him are Sean Brown (left) and Gabe Kahaleuahi. November 4, 2006. (Gary T. Kubota)

Above: The sixty-fifth anniversary of the attack of Pearl Harbor is observed by the veterans and their families visiting the USS *Arizona* Memorial. Pearl Harbor survivor Anthony Rella (eighty-eight) shakes hands with every sailor as he nears the entrance to the USS *Arizona* Memorial. November 5, 2006. (Dennis Oda)

Left: The 170th anniversary of the birth of King David Kalakaua was celebrated at Iolani Palace. During the King's Concert Hula program, (from left) Beverley Among, Ginger Yong, Clara Kekahuna, Ana Newsome, Maggie Keener and Harriet Smith listen to the music by the Royal Hawaiian Band. November 16, 2006. (Dennis Oda)

Right: Chris Shivers rides atop Chili moments before getting injured during the Professional Bull Riders' All-Star Challenge at the Blaisdell Arena. November 16, 2006. (Jamm Aquino)

Above: President George W. Bush meets with the military at Camp Smith for breakfast and a briefing. On the way, about three motorcycle cops skid off the rain slick road and crash as they provide traffic control for the Presidential motorcade. November 21, 2006. (Dennis Oda)

Right: Hans Hedemann and his son, Johann, fifteen, pose for a portrait at Queen's Surf Beach in Waikiki. November 23, 2006. (Cindy Ellen Russell)

Left: The playroom at Doggie Day Care Ohana and Spa is a busy place; it can accommodate nearly one hundred dogs. November 24, 2006. (George F. Lee)

Below left: Actress Kelly Hu at the Miss Sixty store in Ala Moana Center. December 2, 2006. (F.L. Morris)

Below: Tree Lighting Ceremony at Honolulu Hale. December 2, 2006. (F.L. Morris)

Below: Aaliyah Huertas, three, follows her mother's lead while performing Puerto Rican folkloric dance during the Hawaii's Plantation Village Celebration of Rice event held in Waipahu. December 6, 2006. (Cindy Ellen Russell)

Right: Mermaids Hawaii makes an accordion formation at the Kalihi District Park pool. December 3, 2006. (Cindy Ellen Russell)

Right: The members of the Royal Order of Kamehameha I lead the procession of Governor Linda Lingle's inaugural party. Governor Lingle and Lieutenant Governor Duke Aiona pause at steps of Iolani Palace. December 4, 2006. (Craig T. Kojima)

Left: The Rainbow Wahine celebrate after a victorious game five over USC in the NCAA Playoffs at the Stan Sheriff Center. December 8, 2006. (Jamm Aquino)

Below: Lynn and Mal Shiroma sit amongst the thousands of stuffed animals Lynn has collected over the years by playing claw games at establishments throughout the island. The Shiromas plan on giving some of the toys to needy children this holiday season. December 12, 2006. (Jamm Aquino)

Right: These horses seek shelter from the sun and rain under this huge tree that's between Haleiwa and Waimea Bay. December 14, 2006. (Dennis Oda)

Below: Don Ho, seated, with Haumea Hebenstreit (left), State Senator Clayton Hee, Lynn Waters, Clay Naluai and Sam Kapu at the Sheraton Waikiki. December 15, 2006. (John Berger)

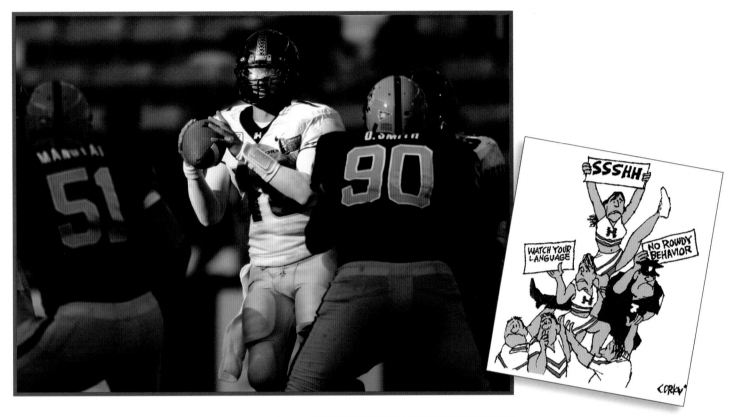

Above left: Hawaii's Colt Brennan searches for an open receiver during first-half action of the Sheraton Hawaii Bowl at Aloha Stadium. December 24, 2006. (Jamm Aquino)

Left: Jonah Featheran sprints down Kailua Beach with a pit bull named Bula. December 20, 2006. (Cindy Ellen Russell)

Right: A paddler for Punahou School's ILH outrigger canoe paddling team, Keegan Wada sits on the wall next to paddles, waiting his turn during practice in the Ala Wai Channel. December 27, 2006. (F.L. Morris)

Below: Rachel Logan, a visitor from Arkansas, lays at the water's edge of Kuhio Beach. It is a beautiful, clear day in paradise. December 24, 2006. (F.L. Morris)

Right: Both children and their parents marvel at balloons dropping from the ceiling during the New Year at Noon festivities at the Hawaii Children's Discovery Center in Kakaako. December 31, 2006. (Jamm Aquino)

Left: George Lu, nine, peers from behind a firework he sets off in Palolo Valley. Lu is celebrating New Year's Eve with his parents Andrew and Kathy and his little brother Jonathan. December 31, 2006. (Cindy Ellen Russell)

Below: Amy Landau before Doris Duke's guesthouse, which is known as the Playhouse and was modeled on the seventeenth-century Persian palace Chehel Sutun (Forty Columns) in Isfahan, Iran. January 4, 2007. (Craig T. Kojima)

Top: Wakako Yamamoto is a tattoo artist at the Hart and Huntington Tattoo Company in Waikiki. January 5, 2007. (Richard Walker)

Above: Eddie Sherman and Elvis (Ron Short) at MAC 24-7. January 8, 2007. (John Berger)

Right: Charlene Biacan, seven, shows intensity while performing basic Kihon during a karate demonstration held at the Hawaii's Plantation Village Celebration of Rice. Biacan is a member of the Ken Shu Kan dojo. January 7, 2007. (Cindy Ellen Russell)

Left: The International Marketplace on Kalakaua Avenue in Waikiki. January 22, 2007. (Richard Walker)

Below: Aerial of the Royal Hawaiian Hotel in Waikiki. January 11, 2007. (Cindy Ellen Russell)

Above: The Mililani High varsity cheerleading squad takes first place for large schools in the 2007 HHSAA Cheerleading Championship at Stan Sheriff Center. January 21, 2007. (Richard Walker)

Right: 171st anniversary of Queen Emma's birthday. These are some of the Saint Andrew's Priory students escorting the picture of Queen Emma to the Royal Crypt. January 23, 2007. (Dennis Oda)

Left: Across from the Crouching Lion Inn, these rocks are piled and balanced on each other. Michael Abreu (owner of Michael's, a restaurant at the Crouching Lion) tells people it's the menehunes that do it, but the real cause is most likely Japanese tourists. January 24, 2007. (Dennis Oda)

Below left: A group of students from Hiroshima Kengitsu Shonan High School in Japan visits Kamaka Hawaii Inc., ukulele makers. Chris Kamaka, third-generation ukulele builder, shows off a Jake Shimabukuro model. January 23, 2007. (Craig T. Kojima)

Below: Bishop Chikai Yosemori poses in front of the altar in the Honpa Hongwanji Bestuin Temple in Nuuanu. He is the bishop of the largest Buddhist sect in Hawaii, and is about to retire after forty years as a minister. January 29, 2007. (Richard Walker)

Right: Cars that are part of the Hawaii Big Boys Show at the Blaisdell were parked at Mauhalua Bay Beach Park in Hawaii Kai. Owners include Alan Zane (Shelby Daytona Coupe '65, right, front) and (row of cars, right to left) Larry Manuel ('32 Coupe three-window Hi-Boy), Rod Baybayan (GS Shelby Cobra Roadster), Eric Yee (360 Modena Ferrari) and Steve Mix ('02 Saleen Mustang). February 3, 2007. (Dennis Oda)

Below: Sarah Holt paddles her way down the shore at Ala Moana Beach Park. February 4, 2007. (Cindy Ellen Russell)

Left: Champion sumo wrestler Konishiki (Salevaa Atisanoe) holds a shaka pose during a group portrait with the Konishiki Kids at his home in Maile. Konishiki and company are celebrating the ten-year anniversary of the Konishiki Kids Foundation. February 10, 2007. (Cindy Ellen Russell)

Below left: With the Father Damien statue and afternoon traffic in the foreground, a rainbow forms over Punchbowl this afternoon. February 23, 2007. (Richard Walker)

Below: Iolani High School senior wrestler Carla Watase has won three state titles. February 26, 2007. (Richard Walker)

Right: Masu's in Liliha closes for good. Paul Masuoka, the owner, with his "Wall of Fame"—framed photos of his notable customers. February 26, 2007. (Craig T. Kojima)

Below: UH Rainbows vs. Boise State in the Stan Sheriff Center was Coach Riley Wallace's last home game. Coach Wallace was honored for twenty years as head coach of the men's basketball team with a ceremony following the game. March 3, 2007. (F.L. Morris)

Below right: Comedian Andy Bumatai performs at the Esprit Lounge in the Sheraton Waikiki Hotel, marking a return to Waikiki stages for Bumatai after a long break. March 16, 2007. (Jamm Aquino)

Left: After their performance of traditional Chinese folk songs and English nursery rhymes, the China Blue-Sky Children Arts Troupe were given leis made from students from Queen Kaahumanu School and Royal Elementary. March 7, 2007. (Dennis Oda)

Above left: City administration did a walk-through of the Walter Murray Gibson building to justify why it needs to be renovated next fiscal year. March 19, 2007. (Craig T. Kojima)

Above: Marine Corporal Chris Sullivan poses for a portrait at 808 Tattoo in Kaneohe with his wife Stephanie and son Bailey, seven months. Sullivan is at the shop getting work done before the new tattoo restrictions take effect on Sunday. March 29, 2007. (Cindy Ellen Russell)

Right: This person carries her board on her head as she walks down Kalakaua Avenue in Waikiki. April 2, 2007. (Richard Walker)

Above: More than 250 marines of the Second Battalion, Third Marines return home to MCBH Kaneohe after serving seven months in Iraq. Here, Wade and Ashley Mayhew, right, and Alan and Melissa Lee greet each other. April 8, 2007. (Richard Walker)

Right: Zakaria Khairane and his two children, Zahra Khairane (three, left) and her brother Mehdi Khairane (four), cool off with a shower at Ala Moana Beach. April 5, 2007. (Dennis Oda)

Top and left: Ka Pa Hula O Ka Lei Lehua from Nanakuli, Oahu, visit Kilauea to pay their respect to the land and Pele. They dance and offer ho'okupu by throwing their leis into the crater. April 11, 2007. (Dennis Oda)

Above: Keola Dalire prepares her ho'okupu which she will throw into Kilauea Crater. She is the youngest daughter of kumu hula Aloha Dalire. The ohia tree is full of blossoms. April 12, 2007. (Dennis Oda)

Right: Al Davis, Bob Nash, Artie Wilson, and Dwight Holiday (all former UH basketball players) share a laugh after Nash was named UH Basketball head coach. April 13, 2007. (Craig T. Kojima)

Below: Arlene Holzman has won every solo paddling women's competition this year. Holzman will be competing in the Kanaka Ikaika State Championship. April 18, 2007. (Cindy Ellen Russell)

Left: The City takes the contest lei from the May First Annual Lei Day Celebration to Mauna Ala, the Royal Mausoleum. The lei are presented to Na Alii O Hawaii (Hawaiian royalty) in a simple ceremony. May 2, 2007. (Craig T. Kojima)

Above: Like Like was with his two dogs, David (left) and Sheba, at the Food Bank drive when his two dogs decided to give him a good old fashion lickin'. April 21, 2007. (Dennis Oda)

Top: Haumea Hebenstreit, widow of Don Ho, holds the urn containing Don's ashes during ceremonies off Waikiki Beach. May 5, 2007. (Hugh Gentry)

Above left: A farewell card dedicated to Don Ho in the main lobby of the Hilton Hawaiian Village. May 3, 2007. (Cindy Ellen Russell)

Above: Family, friends and well-wishers paddle outrigger canoes, ride boats, surf, or swim to get offshore of Waikiki to lay Don Ho's ashes to rest at sea. May 5, 2007. (Dennis Oda)

This page: Thousands gather at Waikiki Beach for a concert that followed the memorial services for entertainer Don Ho. May 5, 2007. (Richard Walker)

Right: Mililani's D'Andre Benjamin won the 110-meter hurdles with a time of 15.61. Waianae's Kelemeke Maifea and Radford's Christopher Smith flanked him. May 5, 2007. (Cindy Ellen Russell)

Below right: Filipino Fiesta features entertainment, food, business exhibitors, cultural presentations and more at Kapiolani Bandstand. This is Kathleen Antonio-Miyashiro and Derrick Rufo dancing the tinikling, or bamboo dance performed by the Philippine Cultural Group of Hawaii. May 12, 2007. (Dennis Oda)

Above: Danny Bongo demonstrates how to throw a net at Ala Moana Beach. May 16, 2007. (Dennis Oda)

Left: Andy Baldwin and Tessa Horst meet the press and their fans at Moana Hotel in Waikiki. A two-carat ring adorns the hand of Tessa. May 25, 2007. (Craig T. Kojima)

Right: Sumotori from the east side stand before the start of sumo action at Blaisdell Arena. June 9, 2007. (Richard Walker)

Below right: Local kids get a chance to try their hand at wrestling with real sumotori before the start of the sumo action at Blaisdell Arena. This boy isn't doing too well against Kasugao. June 9, 2007. (Richard Walker)

Left: At the Habitat for Humanity build site in Waianae, resident Shantelle Ho'ohuli watches with her four-month-old daughter Shaistin through a window in the newly placed wall of a house. June 16, 2007. (Richard Walker)

Left: Foster children ride horses and interact with farm animals at the Waimanalo Polo Fields. The kids are part of Heart Gallery Hawaii, where volunteer professional photographers photograph foster kids to help get them adopted. This is Chassidy Kruse, eleven, giving her horse a hug. June 29, 2007. (Dennis Oda)

Above: Tears well up in ten-year-old Ivana-Ajee Dolic's eyes as she embraces her father, Seargent Stephen Dolic, during a welcome home ceremony at Wheeler Army Air Base for about two hundred soldiers of the Forty-fifth Sustainment Brigade after one year of deployment in Iraq. July 3, 2007. (Jamm Aquino)

Top. The Hawaii Superferry approached Honolulu Harbor for the first time as seen from Magic Island. June 30, 2007. (Richard Walker)

Right: The Hawaii Superferry Alakai at Pier 19 in the Honolulu Harbor. The 350-foot vessel can carry up to four hundred passengers and 110 vehicles, and is scheduled to start inter-island service from Oahu to Maui and Kauai in late August. June 30, 2007. (Cindy Ellen Russell)

Left: Toby, a blue and gold macaw, takes flight during the Aloha Hawaiian Parrot Association's birthday celebration at Neal Blaisdell Park in Aiea. The Association meets once a month, and members and their parrots enjoy an afternoon of mingling and picnicking. July 8, 2007. (Jamm Aquino)

Left: Mamoru Kodama, owner of Kodama Koi Farms in Mililani, and the Aloha Koi Appreciation Society donated 835 koi to the Hilton Hawaiian Village Beach Resort & Spa. These koi were just released into the pond by the Alii Tower. July 18, 2007. (Dennis Oda)

Above: Garden House, a landmark Honolulu garden supply store operating for more than sixty years, will close its doors in early July. This is the store's sign, a familiar sight at the corner of Piikoi and Beretania Streets. July 3, 2007. (F.L. Morris)

Above: J.J. Augustine gets a cooling-off shower after a enjoying a sunny day at Ala Moana Beach with his family. July 27, 2007. (Dennis Oda)

Right: Hoku Ho is the opening act to Gwen Stefani in concert at the Neil Blaisdell Center. August 24, 2007. (Dennis Oda)

Left: The former Club Hubba Hubba
on North Hotel Street sits vacant
and in disrepair. October 12, 2007.
(Richard Walker)

Above: A woman and her dog ply
the calm morning waters at Ala Moana
Beach. November 22, 2007.
(Richard Walker)

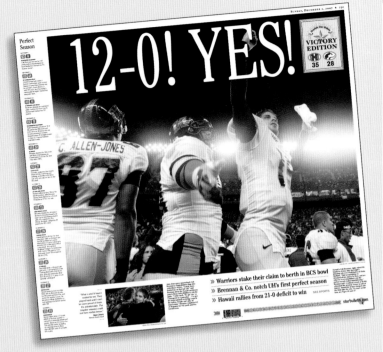

The Perfect Season

The median price range for a home in the Islands might be in the upper-hundreds of thousands of dollars, but at heart this place is blue-collar to the bone. Despite the preponderance of posh neighborhoods, private schools, and wealth aggregated in small conclaves around the state, much of the people who live here must get by solely on will, muscle, and grit—it's a work ethic that has transferred to our sports teams, especially the 2007 University of Hawaii Warrior football team. The 2007 team was dazzling to watch. Led by QB Colt Brennan, the team went 12-0 on their way to their first appearance in the NCAA Bowl Championship Series. Along the way they provided numerous thrills, winning five of their games by a margin of 7 points or less (and 2 of those were in OT), Colt Brennan breaking the NCAA record for most career touchdowns (131), a WAC championship, and the proof that the UH program was every bit as good as its mainland counterparts. The Georgia Bulldogs put an end to the fun at the Sugar Bowl, but that loss didn't diminish all that came before it. This was a team of scrappers who clawed and fought all the way to the top, and they brought all of us along for the ride.

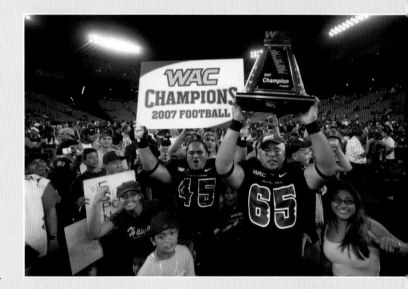

Top: UH coach June Jones talks with QB Colt Brennan during the Boise State game. November 23, 2007. (Dennis Oda)

Above right: UH beats Boise State 39-27 to win the WAC championship. Spencer Smith holds the sign while Hercules Satele lifts the WAC trophy. November 23, 2007. (Dennis Oda)

Right: The Hawaii Warriors cheer after performing the ha'a before the start of the Sugar Bowl at the Superdome in New Orleans. January 1, 2008. (Richard Walker)

Above: A group of native Hawaiians, including Walter Ritte from Molokai, camp on the grounds of Iolani Palace on the eve of the legislative session opening to encourage lawmakers to hear a bill that would end the genetic engineering of taro. Ritte speaks to the media. January 15, 2008. (F.L. Morris)

Left: Roosevelt senior guard Dianna Zane takes her focus and intensity beyond the court and into the gym. January 26, 2008. (Jamm Aquino)

Above: From left, Amber Zufelt, Joy Riddle, Crista Hall, Erik Alves and his cousin, Ian Alves, soak up the sun as they sit at the water's edge at Ala Moana Beach. March 13, 2008. (Dennis Oda)

Right: Japanese tourists pose along the shores of Waikiki at Kuhio Beach Park. From the back to front are Kohei Chiba, Tomoyuki Ikemoto, Takahiro Tanabe, Ichiho Miura, Taichi Nishimura, Yoshihisa Ishikawa, Risa Iwanaga, Satomi Iwamoto, Yukini Arai, Yuka Taguchi, Yukiko Okamuro and Akane Inadomi. They are recent graduates from Nihon University in Tokyo. March 6, 2008. (Cindy Ellen Russell)

Above: The Aloha Airlines ticketing counter at Honolulu International Airport is empty. April 2, 2008. (Cindy Ellen Russell)

Left: Photographed in their home in Nuuanu, the Serrao family are Hawaiian quilt-makers and teach quilt-making workshops. From left to right, Cissy, John and Althea Serrao. April 8, 2008. (F.L. Morris)

Right: At the Stop Rail Now rally at City Hall, Dan Douglas, left, Dennis Callan and Mike Uechi speak against a rail system. April 21, 2008. (Craig T. Kojima)

Below right: Renovations in the Hickam Air Force Base community will begin in a couple of months and will keep the look and feel of the community as it was originally built in the late 1930s and early 40s. Large trees, such as these that lead to the historic water tower near the elementary school, will not be touched. April 24, 2008. (Dennis Oda)

Above: Lydia Mahelona Akamine, left, with all of her Channel 4 supporters. Pamela Young (second from left), Wanda Wehr, John Wray, Gary Sprinkle, Sid Milburn, Tracy Keliihoomalu, and Brent Suyama. April 25, 2008. (Craig T. Kojima)

Left: Newlyweds Yasuhiro and Sato Ohki jumping for joy at Ala Moana Beach. April 29, 2008. (Dennis Oda)

Above: At the HOT studio in Kakaako, dancer Malia Yamamoto takes part in a dress rehearsal of the Iona Contemporary Dance Theater's upcoming performance, "Paint by Number." May 5, 2008. (F.L. Morris)

Right: On Mother's Day about forty children visit their mothers and grand-mothers, who are housed at the Women's Community Correctional Center. Inmates, their children, and Momi Akana (the Executive Director of Keiki O Ka Aina Family Learning Center, pictured wearing a green shirt) take part in a "tug-of-war" with other mothers and children. Later in the day, U.S. Marines give out toys to children visiting the center. May 10, 2008. (Dennis Oda)

Left: Lanterns carrying messages and prayers float out to sea at the 10th annual *Toro Nagashi*. May 26, 2008 (Richard Walker)

Below: Lanterns are launched off Ala Moana Beach Park during the May 2008 floating lantern ceremonies, known as *Toro Nagashi*. May 26, 2008. (F.L. Morris)

Sophie Gatewood, left, and Mahealani Carvalho, greeters at Hilo Hattie's on Nimitz Highway, stand before the world's largest aloha shirt. June 2, 2008. (Craig T. Kojima)

Left: Snowie, a two-year-old Shiba Inu, cares for her surrogate "pups"—four kittens abandoned by their mother— in the living room of Frank Schultz's Iroquois Point home. Schultz and his wife discovered the kittens in their woodshed and began caring for them, feeding them with an eye-dropper. Snowie eventually took over for her owners by letting the kittens feed from her teats. June 3, 2008. (Jamm Aquino)

Below: From right, Chris and Genie Kincaid stand with their daughter, Rachel, fourteen, after a day out in their canoes. The Kincaids are passionate about their paddling, both individually and as a family. June 10, 2008. (Jamm Aquino)

Right: At Mokuleia Beach Park homeless campers face a looming eviction deadline. With her possessions packed and her tent dismantled, Marie Beltran, shown here holding her granddaughter, Kanoe Keawemauhili, ponders an uncertain future. June 16, 2008. (F.L. Morris)

Below: Former *American Idol* star Jasmine Trias performs with SOS LV. The band is in town for a run of nightly shows at the Outrigger Hotel's main showroom. June 27, 2008. (Jamm Aquino)

Left: At Lex Brodie's on Queen Street, drivers line up for gas, which is about six cents cheaper per gallon when paid with cash. June 27, 2008. (Craig T. Kojima)

Below: Professional surfer C. J. Kanuha rides his stand-up paddle board off the Big Island's southeastern coast where the lava was hitting the ocean. April, 2008. (Kirk Aeder)

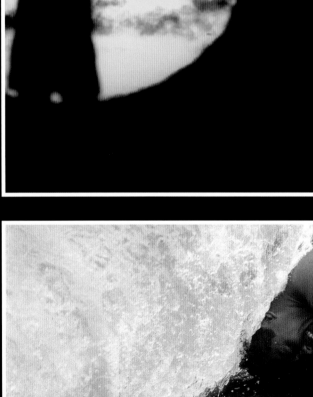

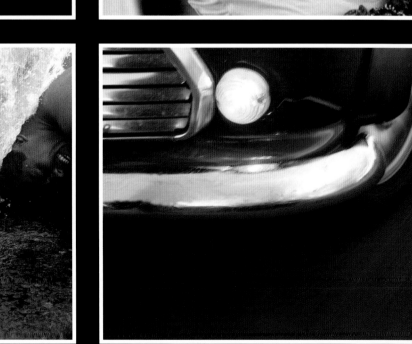

PHOTOGRAPHERS' CHOICE

This book chronicles fifty years of newspaper photography. Over these fifty years, newspaper photography has been totally transformed. Photography was once analog: exposed physical film was processed with chemicals to make negatives which were then printed. Now it's all done with computers. The camera is digital; the editing is digital. The newest technology allows nearly everyone to become a photographer. Producing passable pictures before digital cameras required a very specialized set of skills ranging from the knowledge of light and films to chemistry.

But some things have remained the same. A good photojournalist still has to catch the moment: revealing a story while being visually appealing. The newspaper, whether it's ink on newsprint or pixels on a screen, has to be trustworthy. The photos still illustrate as well as complement the story for the reader.

Not Necessarily the Good Old Days

Many contemporary photojournalists started taking pictures in the days of gelatin film and wet labs. They shot with larger format cameras and then, as technology changed, in 35mm, calculating exposure, focus, and color balance on the fly. Then it was all about speed: the film had to be rushed to the office and developed quickly, to be featured on the front page a few hours later.

The old pros had their tricks. *Star-Bulletin* photographer Craig Kojima reminisced about a two-man team working on a tight deadline. After

shooting the film and leaving the scene, one photographer drove while the other started to develop the film. Once at the office, the photos were enlarged and prepared for press. All this in less than 30 minutes.

In the old days the photos were "dodged and burned" to emphasize or de-emphasize certain portions of a print, making one portion lighter or darker than the rest. But it took time and skill and simple tools like your hands.

The actual newspaper pages were composed on boards placed upon "turtles," where text galleys and printed photos were waxed into place. A large copy camera took actual-size negatives, the basis for the printing plates used to print the newspaper.

Photos were stored for possible future use, which took a lot of space. The *Star-Bulletin's* photo print archives once occupied an entire room. There were bookcases six feet high with each shelf loaded with folders organized alphabetically.

Brave New World

Now a photo is an electronic file composed of ones and zeros, taken with a digital camera and edited with Photoshop. Professional newspaper photographers are experts at handling digital cameras, which have freed them from worrying about light, exposure, f-stops, and shutter speeds, allowing them to concentrate on capturing the moment. The process is so simple that even the reporters now carry point-and-shoot digital cameras, blurring the line between writer and photographer. Digital technology has brought an egalitarianism to many newsrooms.

Because the photo is digital, it can be sent over the Net. No more rushing physical film to the newspaper offices. Nowadays, the photographer will transfer the files from the digital camera to the laptop for viewing and an initial sort. The photos can then be compressed and sent to the photo desk by email.

At the office, the photo is cataloged into a central server used by editors and page designers. The editor picks the photos to be used, and with the page designer they decide whether photos for the newsprint edition will run in color or black and white, and at what size. Then the photo desk processes the photos accordingly, correcting for exposure, balancing colors, sharpening, and resizing and converting to printer's colors. The processed photo is then sent back to the page designer where it is placed into the electronic layout that will become the printed page.

Online editions of newspapers remove some of the limitations imposed by the earlier printing process, as there is no need to convert a photo to black and white, or to reduce it in size. The Web is a limitless landscape of media, unfettered by the rising cost of newsprint, limitations of a printing press, and old-style delivery systems.

As in the old days, photos are still archived. However, storage no longer requires a room full of shelves and folders. Now pictures are stored on computer servers. Even the old analog photos are being converted: strips of negatives in sleeves are scanned and the resulting digital files kept on DVDs.

New Technology and the Photographer

Photoshop is the new enlarger in the digital darkroom. It is a powerful tool that performs nearly all of the technical tasks once done in the old chemical darkroom. Cellular telephones and PC cards with cellular telephony, in conjunction with our laptop computers and the Internet,

bridge the distances between photographers in the field and editors in the newsroom. The latest digital cameras now have settings that not only handle for exposure, but allow the user to set color preferences, record a voice message, use global positioning systems, record in more than one format, and send to more than one location. The very newest of accessories also allows a wireless and effortless transfer of images directly to the laptop computer for editing and transmission.

More Change in the Future

Every generation of print journalists has had to contend with advances in technology and changes that redefine how both writers and photographers work. Digital tools, like digital cameras and Photoshop, have simplified the preparation of the printed newspaper. Now the latest digital tool, the Internet, is pushing newspapers towards a predominantly paperless medium.

This is blurring the lines between media. Online newspapers commonly feature photo essays in the form of audio slide slows. Newspapers show video clips, erasing the line between newspapers and television. Photojournalists learn videography and do voiceovers—their work is no longer limited to the confines of the printed pages. Some photographers have even become bloggers and online columnists. Many of the *Star-Bulletin* writers, editors, and photographers are now the new columnists in cyberspace.

The following portfolio showcases selected work by each of our seven current staff photograhers.

George F. Lee
Photography Editor
Honolulu Star-Bulletin

Jamm AQUINO

"The most difficult part of the job is drawing that line between being a journalist and being a human that we all are, especially when I'm photographing delicate subjects. There have been times where I just had to put the camera down out of respect."

Top: Hawaii quarterback Colt Brennan raises a finger after capturing the 2007 WAC title. November 23, 2007.

Above: 1968 Austin Rover Mini Cooper. July 25, 2006

Right: UH Wahine Volleyball senior Julianna Sanders is an avid surfer and skateboarder outside the volleyball court. August 7, 2007.

Craig KOJIMA

"The job is exciting. But it is just what we do. Sometimes it can become mystical, when fate conspires to give you a special photograph. At one time, I believe that photographers were truly magicians."

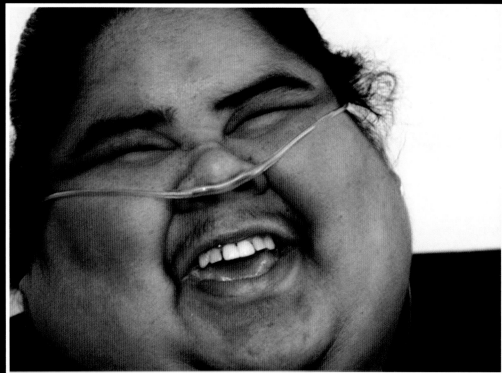

Top: Sio Saipia, left, Pele Baker and Bob Jendins play on a Waikiki Beach wall. October 10, 1999.

Above: "Izzy" was laughing while I shot as many photos as I wanted. May 17, 1996.

Left: Cheo Kojima, my daughter and "Mango."

George F. LEE

"This job has helped me become a master of the short-term relationship. Often we have only a few minutes to get to know someone and get on with the photography. Having a few hours to spend is a rarity."

Top: Helicopters fly a missing man formation during candle ceremonies at Punchbowl on Sunday. May 25, 2003.

Above: Puppet makers stall, Mandalay. March 3, 2001.

Right: Nainoa Thompson and the Hokulea at sunset. April 24, 1999.

F. L. MORRIS

"Photographers needing a good sense of ESP, understanding–following a sense that I believe man lost when he developed speech. Like fishing–it is good to be lost yet taking the right fork in the road intuitively. Finding your spot."

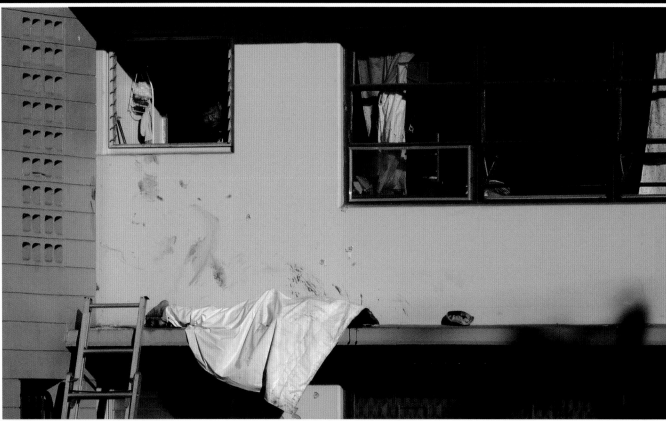

Top: Three guys in a barrel at Ala Moana Bowls. April 26, 2004.

Above: HPD officer looks out the window at a victim of a shooting. June 17, 2004.

Right: Iona dance rehearsal.

Cindy Ellen RUSSELL

"There are dangers with the job, too. Murderers being pursued, helicopters flying past erupting volcanoes, circus animals on a rampage. These are all exceptions, but they do happen and we are expected to be there."

Top: Jason Scott Lee at his Volcano home on the Big Island, Hawaii. July 29, 2005.

Above: Kalaupapa patient Norbert Palea and top side Molokai resident Pearl Keawe sang a mele while waiting for a departing flight at the airport. May 10, 2008

Dennis ODA

"You have to get along with people so you can get closer to the story. If you don't have access, you don't get good pictures. This is much more than just a job."

Top: Lisa Jimenez tests the calm waters off Ala Moana Beach after sunset. December 20, 1998.

Above left: Schoen Safotu and his wife, Nenny Safotu light candles during a service for the victims of the terrorist attacks. September 13, 2001.

Above: A dancer from Keolalaulani Halau 'Olapa 'O Laka at the Merrie Monarch. April 14, 1986.

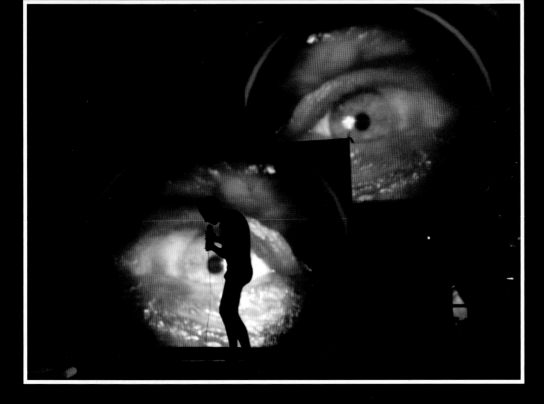

Richard WALKER

"You need the skills of every type of photographer out there; Be able to sweet talk your way into weird situations, and then sweet talk your way out. Half the time I think I'm more of a psychologist with a camera."

Top: A silhoutte of *Tool* vocalist Maynard James Keenan at Andrews Ampitheater. November 1, 2001.

Left: Partial solar eclipse at Magic Island. October 13, 2004.

Above: "Ruthless" Robbie Lawler, left, gets a hit on Frank "Twinkle Toes" Trigg. March 31, 2007.

CHRONOLOGY

1950

April 1—The House Un-American Activities Committee, holding hearings at 'Iolani Palace to investigate alleged Communist infiltration of the labor movement, issues subpoenas to seventy people, of whom thirty-nine refuse to testify. The "Reluctant 39" are charged with contempt of Congress, but the U.S. Supreme Court later throws out the charges.

June 25—North Korea invades South Korea. An estimated 17,000 Hawaiian residents serve in the conflict, in which 341 are killed and another 79 are recorded as missing in action. The war ends on July 27, 1953.

1951

August 28—Seven union organizers are indicted for violating the Smith Act, which criminalized advocating the use of force or violence to overthrow the U.S. government. Their conviction in 1953 leads to an all-Island walkout of union members. The verdict is overturned in 1958 after the U.S. Supreme Court rules that the teaching of Communism is not illegal.

1952

July—Three Hawaiian residents win gold medals in the Helsinki Olympics: William Woolsey (800-meter freestyle relay), Ford Konno (1,500-meter freestyle), and Yoshio Oyakawa (100-meter backstroke).

December 1—KGMB becomes the first television station in Hawai'i to air a scheduled broadcast.

1953

From Here to Eternity, James Jones' novel, is filmed on O'ahu.

1954

February 10—The people of Hawai'i sign a petition to Congress asking for statehood.

1955

Pineapple production in the Islands peaks with 76,700 acres planted.

March 22—The worst air disaster in Hawai'i's history occurs when a military transport plane crashes in the Wai'anae Mountains, killing all sixty-six passengers.

September 26—The Latter Day Saints Church College of Hawai'i is established in Lā'ie. Dedicated in 1958, it becomes a branch campus of Brigham Young University, Provo, in 1974.

1956

September—The Waikīkī Shell opens.

1957

Waikīkī's International Marketplace opens.

January 9—North Vietnam formally announces its support for Communist guerillas in South Vietnam, thus beginning the Vietnam War, which lasts until 1975. Of 13,000 Hawaiian residents who take part in the war, 221 die in hostile action, and another 51 from war-related events.

March 9—An earthquake in the Aleutian Islands generates a tsunami that destroys seventy-five homes on Kaua'i's north shore.

May 11—The first two tunnels on the Pali Highway open to one-way traffic. All four lanes open to two-way traffic on August 1, 1961.

1958

August 31—The Matson Navigation Company's cargo ship *Hawaiian Merchant* ushers in container shipping between the West Coast and Kaua'i.

1959

Kaiser Hospital opens.

March 12—The U.S. Congress passes a bill approving Hawai'i's admission into the Union of States.

July 3—President John F. Kennedy arrives in Honolulu and delivers a speech to the Teamsters Union.

August 3—The Ala Moana Shopping Center, then only 50 acres, opens.

August 6—Hurricane Dot lashes Kaua'i with winds of more than 100 miles per hour, causing $20 million in damage.

August 21—President Eisenhower signs the Statehood Proclamation, admitting Hawai'i officially as the fiftieth state. On July 4, 1960, a fiftieth star is added to the flag of the United States, Republican William Quinn becomes Hawai'i's first state governor, and Daniel Inouye is elected to the U.S. House of Representatives, becoming Hawai'i's first Congressman and the first Japanese American in either the U.S. House or Congress.

August 21—James Michener publishes his novel *Hawaii,* which he finished on the day that Congress approved Hawaiian statehood.

November 14—Kīlauea Iki (Little Kīlauea) displays a stunning fire show when fountains of lava erupt to heights of 1,900 feet, the highest ever recorded in the Islands.

1960

May 22—A large earthquake centered near Chile generates a tsunami that arrives in Hawai'i fifteen hours later on the morning of May 23. It creates a bore that rushes ashore in Hilo Bay over a 4-mile section of the waterfront, sending water up to 36 feet above sea level and killing sixty one people.

July—The East-West Center is established at the University of Hawai'i to "strengthen understanding and relations between the United States and the countries of the Asia Pacific region."

1961

April—Elvis Presley begins filming *Blue Hawaii,* in which he sings the "Hawaiian Wedding Song." The famous wedding scene takes place in a canoe in the lagoon at Kaua'i's Coco Palms Hotel.

April 7—James Michener, author of *Hawaii,* stirs up a storm of controversy with claims of racial discrimination.

1962

Singer Don Ho performs at Duke's in Waikīkī on his way to becoming one of the most widely known musicians from the Islands. He releases his first album in 1965 and, along with his biggest hit, "Tiny Bubbles," he becomes a staple of the Waikīkī music scene for the next forty years.

May 31—The U.S.S. *Arizona* Memorial is dedicated at Pearl Harbor; it is positioned directly over the wreck of the U.S.S. *Arizona.*

July 9—A nuclear bomb is detonated 800 miles from Hawai'i at Johnston Island, lighting up the Hawaiian sky.

October 6—The *Sigma 7* spacecraft, after circling Earth six times with Astronaut Walter M. Schirra on board, plunges into the Pacific Ocean about 1,300 miles north of Honolulu. The aircraft carrier *Kearsarge* picks up Schirra, who is then flown to O'ahu's Hickam Air Force Base.

November 7—Democrat John A. Burns is elected governor of Hawai'i, defeating Republican incumbent William Quinn. His victory marks the first time local Democrats control both the executive and legislative branches of the state's government. Daniel K. Inouye joins Hiram L. Fong as the first U.S. Senate members of Asian ancestry.

1963

John Dominis Holt writes the essay "On Being Hawaiian," considered by many to be a seminal work inspiring a cultural reawakening that will come to be known as the Hawaiian Renaissance.

June 9—President John F. Kennedy, speaking at the National Conference of Mayors in Honolulu, urges attendees to help calm the civil rights crisis.

October 12—The Polynesian Cultural Center opens in Lāʻie, Oʻahu.

1964

The Honolulu International Center opens. It comprises a sports arena complex, exhibit hall, and auditorium. The site is renamed the Neal S. Blaisdell Center in 1976.

March 27—One of the largest earthquakes ever recorded in North America occurs in Alaska. It registers a magnitude of 8.4 on the Richter scale and generates tsunami waves that cause flooding in Kahului, Maui, and Hilo.

April—The Merrie Monarch Festival premieres in Hilo.

1966

Fewer than 1,000 Humpback whales are estimated to remain from a pre-whaling population of 200,000.

The "Lani Bird" satellite, officially known as *Intelsat 2*, broadcasts the Islands' first live television show from the U.S. mainland.

Sugar production in the Islands peaks at 1,234,121 tons.

November 7—William S. Richardson is appointed Chief Justice of the Hawaiʻi Supreme Court by Governor John A. Burns. Holding the post until 1982, he leads an activist court that significantly expands native Hawaiian rights as well as public access to beaches and state waters.

1967

The state of Hawaiʻi's annual visitor count exceeds 1 million people for the first time.

1968

Hawaiʻi Democrats establish the nation's first right-to-strike law for public-employee unions, strengthening a powerful union lobby that begins to significantly influence political activity.

January 22—Duke Kahanamoku—1912 Olympic swimming champion, movie star, sheriff, and Hawaiʻi's official "Ambassador of Aloha"—passes away at the age of seventy-seven. Thousands attend his "Beachboy" funeral ceremony.

November—Frank F. Fasi is elected Mayor of the City and County of Honolulu, beginning the first of five consecutive terms.

November 6—Richard M. Nixon wins the presidential election in a surprise comeback victory.

1969

The Bank of Bishop & Co. Ltd. is renamed First Hawaiian Bank.

March 15—Governor John Burns dedicates the new State Capitol Building in Honolulu.

April 15—Statues of King Kamehameha I and Father Damien are placed in Washington D.C.'s National Statuary Hall, recognizing the two men as United States heroes.

July 24—The Apollo 11 *Columbia 3* space capsule splashes down in the Pacific Ocean after returning from the first human visit to the moon. The astronauts are picked up by the carrier USS *Hornet* and brought to Pearl Harbor where they are greeted by 25,000 people. They are quarantined at Pearl Harbor's Ford Island for three days before being flown to Houston with the space capsule.

1970

Police uncover a gang of criminals, known as "The Syndicate," that controls most of the gambling, narcotics, and prostitution in the Islands. In a crackdown on prostitution, police also learn that about 90 percent of Honolulu prostitutes are from the mainland and work for a group of procurers.

Tony Hodges, a candidate for the U.S. Senate, raises public awareness of various ecological concerns, releasing information

about pollution at the Waipahu dump, oil dumping at the airport and danger from seeping oil tanks on Kauaʻi and the Big Island. At the end of his one-issue campaign, which garners 30,000 votes, Hodges files a suit against the Attorney General and State Health Department. He alleges 183 violations committed by the state, all the Islands' counties, and most of the sugar, pineapple, and electric companies in Hawaiʻi.

In the gubernatorial race, Gov. John A. Burns defeats former Lt. Gov. Thomas P. Gill by 13,000 votes in the primary, and then crushes Republican nominee Judge Samuel P. King by 36,000 votes in the general election. The elections again leave the Democrats in control of the State Senate and House and the four county councils.

October 9—Two thousand hotel workers represented by the ILWU go on a strike lasting seventy-six days in what becomes the largest hotel worker's strike in Hawaiʻi's history.

October 23—State Senator Larry Kuriyama is shot to death near his home in Aiea following a political rally in Pacific Palisades.

December 8—The on-again, off-again merger of Hawaiian Airlines and Aloha Airlines awaits approval by the Civil Aeronautics Board following overwhelming stockholder support of both airlines. The approval is never given.

December 18—An end to the hotel strike nears for 2,000 Neighbor Island workers.

1971

January 1—Transit workers strike against the Honolulu Rapid Transit Company. The strike lasts for two months, inconveniencing 70,000 commuters and leading to the creation of a city transportation system.

July 1—A major strike by West Coast and Hawaiʻi dockworkers begins, with

about 15,000 members stopping work until October of 1971 when President Nixon halts the strike for 90 days. The strike resumes the day after Christmas and continues until February, lasting 134 days in all and resulting in shortages for all manner of goods.

December—The first annual Pipeline Masters surf contest is held on Oʻahu's North Shore.

1972

The annual visitor count of the Hawaiian Islands exceeds 2 million people.

The sugar industry continues its decline as more plantations close. The future of the pineapple industry also seems bleak.

Japanese investors go on a buying spree, even buying the Pearl City Tavern, an iconic local institution. The spree is fueled by the Japanese yen's rise against the dollar.

City consultants recommend a fixed-rail transit system from Pearl City to Hawaiʻi Kai, while an Interdepartmental Transportation Control Commission is established to limit automobile use.

In politics, Democrats squabble as a springtime fight for party control unfolds. The state announces that it is broke, leading Governor Burns to put a freeze on new programs and most state hiring. Despite these developments, Hawaiʻi voters decide to keep incumbent state Democrats in office. For the first time in state history, however, these same voters give their support to a Republican presidential candidate.

Life of the Land environmentalists win a court order halting progress on the H-3 highway across the Koʻolau Mountains, but they lose a court battle to stop the state's reef runway at International Airport.

A Kauaʻi homesteader holds fifty National Guardsmen under citizen's arrest for trespassing on his Hawaiian homestead land.

January—At Oʻahu's Ota Camp, Americans of Filipino descent organize to fight for government intervention before development wipes out their community. A largely Hawaiian group at Kahaluʻu resists development and protests the destruction of traditional country lifestyles.

1973

An influx of tourists from Japan begins.

The crime rate continues to climb, as violent, unprovoked attacks on tourists go on the upswing. The murder rate inside Oʻahu prisons soars; the National Guard moves in to restore order. However, some notorious crime figures are hauled into court and convicted.

The legislature passes measures to reform campaign finance laws, institute no-fault car insurance, and keep the doors closed to commercial gambling.

Hawaiʻi's Supreme Court hands down two sweeping decisions that put water usage and increased beach access in the public domain.

Chief Justice William S. Richardson declares in the *McBryde Sugar Company v. Robinson* court case that water supplies must remain within their originating watershed.

January 14—Elvis Presley performs at the Honolulu International Center in his *Aloha From Hawaiʻi* concert, broadcast live via satellite to an estimated 1.5 billion people worldwide.

March 29—American troop involvement in the Vietnam War ends and U.S. prisoners of war come home.

April 3—Two large labor unions go on strike: teachers and electrical utility employees. Both strikes have upbeat endings as mediation-arbitration is accepted as an innovative new means of settling intractable labor-management standoffs.

April 26—A magnitude-6.2 earthquake in Hilo causes an estimated $1 million of damage throughout the Islands.

May 20—Former Attorney-General Mitchell claims no wrongdoing in the

Watergate scandal. In the ensuing federal investigation, Hawaiʻi Senator Daniel K. Inouye becomes known to Americans as a Watergate investigator. Mitchell is convicted two years later.

December 16—The first Honolulu Marathon is held. Out of 162 entrants, 151 finish. The race eventually becomes one of the largest of its kind in the world.

1974

The state ends hospitalization for leprosy. Later in the year, conditions at state institutions for the mentally ill and mentally retarded come under attack by national authorities.

Wrangling over a fixed guideway system for Honolulu continues. The reef runway is given a green light by the courts; the H-3 freeway gets partial approval.

January 25—The energy crisis sees Island motorists lining up at service stations. The state's GASPLAN eases the crisis, helping reduce the chaos of gasoline lines and ultimately avoiding rationing.

October 7—George R. Ariyoshi becomes the first U.S. governor of Japanese-American ancestry.

December 11—The Pentagon decides to shut down Hawaiʻi's Army and Air Force Pacific-wide commands.

1975

Commercial whale-watching trips to view humpback whales begin in Hawaiian waters, first off Maui and then around all the major Hawaiian islands.

Hawaiʻi welcomes the state visits of President Ford, England's Queen Elizabeth, and Japan's Emperor Hirohito.

The Sugar Act expires, ending quotas and tariffs that had maintained U.S. sugar prices, and eventually causing the shutdown of many of Hawaiʻi's plantations.

January—Waikīkī's hotels continue to be plagued by overbookings. Some would-be Waikīkī tourists are diverted to the Neighbor Islands.

The Honolulu Police Department recruits its first two women police officers.

January 1—Five hours of continuous, sharp earthquakes rock the Big Island, signaling that the Kīlauea Volcano's six-hour eruption the previous day has more in store for island residents.

February—Hawaiian groups begin mobilizing their forces in an attempt to get Congress to give them $1 billion in reparations for lands allegedly taken by the U.S. government.

Governor George R. Ariyoshi, finishing his first term in office, faces persistent criticism of his management of the Kohala Task Force, which is intended to stimulate new industries in North Kohala on Hawaiʻi Island. He accuses the news media of trying to sabotage the task force. He also faces Waikīkī development issues, a political challenge from Lt. Gov. Nelson K. Doi, and a state surplus of $83.4 million that has been committed to projects that are not his priority.

February 10—The National Guard is called in to restore order at the antiquated Hawaiʻi State Prison on Dillingham Boulevard after it is taken over by prisoners.

April 8—Former Gov. John A. Burns, sixty-six, debilitated from his long battle with cancer, passes away.

July 6—Mauna Loa erupts for the first time in twenty-five years; the eruption ends as suddenly as it began.

August 16—"Hawaiʻi Calls," a radio show popular with Islanders and mainlanders for forty years, ends due to high production costs.

September 12—Aloha Stadium opens in Honolulu.

November 29—Two strong earthquakes shake the southeast region of Hawaiʻi Island, generating a localized tsunami that kills two people near a Halapē campground.

December—A United Airlines strike cuts deeply into tourist revenue and puts a solid dent in Hawaiʻi's farming industry by cutting off shipments to mainland markets.

1976

The sugar industry, a mainstay of the

state economy, finds itself vulnerable to a plunge in retail prices in the wake of the Sugar Act's expiration. The industry mounts a campaign to persuade Congress to restore legislative protection, and gets the backing of the state government, the counties, and organized labor.

Alfred Ruis is re-tried for and acquitted of the murder of Hawaiʻi Senator Larry Kuriyama. Ruis dies from a kidney ailment two weeks after the acquittal. After losing the case, City Prosecutor Maurice Sapienza comes under fire and, late in the year, fails to be reappointed by Mayor Frank Fasi.

January 4—Hawaiian activists begin efforts to release the island of Kahoʻolawe from naval use. They land on the island to dramatize their demands for an end to its use as a bombing target and its return to the Hawaiian people.

June 4—The voyaging canoe *Hōkūleʻa* completes its first round-trip to Tahiti, demonstrating that ancient Polynesians could purposefully navigate the Pacific. The canoe is welcomed by enthusiastic crowds in Papeete and Honolulu.

July—The stylish Hyatt Regency opens as the visitor industry posts its first 3 million-visitor year.

November—The general election results in a serious setback for Hawaiʻi's Republican Party in Hawaiʻi, as former Governor William Quinn and State Rep. Fred Rohlfing lose their battles for congressional seats. The election also sees the retirement of Senator Hiram Fong and the defeat of longtime fixture Rep. Patsy Mink, beaten by Spark Matsunaga in a run for the Democratic nomination for Fong's seat. Meanwhile, Daniel Akaka and Cecil Heftel are sent to Washington to fill congressional vacancies there. Honolulu mayor Frank Fasi is re-elected despite a storm of allegations arising from contracts for furnishing a city-fostered private housing project, Kukui Plaza.

1977

Kīlauea Volcano erupts spectacularly on the Big Island. One of the resulting lava flows points straight toward the village of Kalapana, whose residents are evacuated and watch helplessly as the molten rock advances on their town. Amazingly, the lava stops about three-quarters of a mile from downtown Kalapana.

Honolulu becomes the 13th largest city in the country, and for the first time the population of "rural" O'ahu exceeds that of the "urban" parts of the island. The gross state product is estimated at $7.9 billion, $.8 billion more than last year.

Two assistants at a University of Hawai'i facility release two research dolphins, then try to make the case an issue of animal rights. When brought to trial, the judge says that the question is of theft, not dolphin liberation, and the pair is found guilty.

City planners and the Campbell Estate, owners of the former sugarcane land, envision the southwest O'ahu region of Kapolei as a second major metropolitan center. Kapolei is O'ahu's fastest growing town. There is increasing commercial development and many new projects are planned or in progress, including: a University of Hawai'i West O'ahu campus; state court complex; subdivisions; and hundreds of new condominiums.

January 3—Following a long-standing dispute, residents of Waiahole Valley learn that they will not, after all, be evicted from their homes to make room for a subdivision. Gov. George Ariyoshi agrees to buy Waiahole Valley for $6 million.

March—Honolulu mayor Frank Fasi and his campaign treasurer, Harry Chung, are indicted for bribery. Developer Hal Hansen turns state witness, only to decide later not to testify at the trial that his grand jury testimony has brought about. Hansen also files, and then drops, a $25 million lawsuit against numerous state officials, including Gov. George Ariyoshi. In December all charges against Fasi and Chung are dropped. Prosecutor Grant Cooper marks the dismissal of charges by saying that he has no doubt the mayor is guilty of bribery as charged, adding that it would be "the crime of the century" if Fasi ends up being elected to the governorship.

March 9—George Jarrett Helm Jr. and James "Kimo" Mitchell disappear during their attempt to reclaim the island of Kaho'olawe for native Hawaiians.

1978

Both 'Iolani Luahine, the foremost authority on ancient Hawaiian chants and dances, and Rosalie Lokalia Montgomery,

a leading authority on ancient Hawai'i ways, pass away.

The Nā Hōkū Hanohano Awards are established to recognize excellence in the recording arts in Hawai'i.

Leprosy patients at the state-maintained Hale Mohalu facility in Pearl City refuse to be moved to Leahi Hospital. The state declares the facility a firetrap and health hazard, but patients cling to it as their home.

Operation Green Harvest, a joint federal-state-county anti-marijuana effort, nets more than 17 tons of marijuana valued at $7 million. The House Select Committee on Narcotics Abuse and Control conclude that Hawai'i has become a major waypoint for the movement of illegal drugs.

Hawai'i's de facto population, which measures all those physically present in the state, reaches 984,900. The state's resident population totals 777,300.

February 18—The first Ironman Triathlon competition includes a 2.4-mile ocean swim, a 112-mile bike race, and a 26.2-mile marathon. Tens of thousands of spectators line the route to watch the televised race.

March 16—The *Hōkūle'a* voyaging canoe capsizes in large swells and gale-force winds about twelve miles off Lāna'i, forcing the crew's fifteen members to cling to the canoe's overturned hull. Eddie Aikau volunteers to paddle his surfboard toward Lāna'i for help and disappears. His heroism inspires a local saying: "Eddie would go."

July—A Constitutional Convention convenes for sixty-four days, resulting in, among other things, a "Hawaiian affairs package." In an effort to help preserve Hawaiian society and re-affirm native Hawaiian rights, the package includes amendments to promote the study of Hawaiian culture, history, and language in public schools, to fund the Department of Hawaiian Home Lands with 30 percent of state receipts from water licenses or the lease of sugar lands, and to establish an Office of Hawaiian Affairs to administer reparations granted native Hawaiians.

August—Waiahole Valley residents stage a demonstration at the State Capitol, an event that results in another round of eviction notices.

September—The movement to make reparations to native Hawaiians suffers a setback when the U.S. House of Representatives defeats a proposal to create a commission to determine whether native Hawaiians deserve payments for lands seized by the U.S. government during the 1893 overthrow of the Hawaiian monarchy.

October—Governor George R. Ariyoshi is re-elected to his second full term, defeating Mayor Frank F. Fasi in the primary. In November's general election he soundly beats Republican candidate John Leopold, spending a record $1.7 million in his campaign.

1979

The annual visitor count of the Hawaiian Islands increases to more than 4 million people.

At Sand Island, confrontation ensues between unauthorized Native Hawaiian homesteaders and the state.

Kāne'ohe Base officials report forty-six assaults against Kāne'ohe Marines in the first half of 1979. In Kailua, a Kāne'ohe Marine is shot to death and another wounded as they are heading back to base, and in June another shooting occurs involving Kailua youths and Marines. At an Ewa Beach shopping center, military dependents scuffle with local youths. In July, a rock-throwing mob battles with military police at a Wai'anae military recreation center, and three soldiers are beaten along the highway in Nānākuli while trying to prevent a purse snatching.

A group of ten or more young men rape a Finnish visitor whom they had befriended at Nānākuli Beach.

President Jimmy Carter stops at Hickam Air Force Base for ninety minutes on his way back to Washington from the Tokyo economic summit and talks with ill-fated South Korean president Park Chung Hee.

December—The U.S. Supreme Court rules in a Hawai'i civil case for the first time in a decade, giving the owners of the Hawai'i Kai Marina the right to keep

the waterway private, a decision that has the potential to affect similar questions over public rights of access.

December 8—Both the UH Mānoa and UH Hilo women's volleyball teams win national championships.

1980

The television series *Hawai'i Five-O,* starring Jack Lord as Steve McGarrett, ends after twelve seasons. The show was the first network series to be filmed only in Hawai'i, and was also the longest-running crime drama.

Hawai'i is confronted with a crime and public relations problem that impacts the already shaky tourism industry. In January, a Canadian family vacationing in Kaua'i is brutally attacked by a gang of unknown men while camping in Lydgate Park. When the family returns to Canada, their story of violence is picked up with a vengeance by the Canadian news media and spread worldwide. National and international attention is again leveled on Hawai'i following the December 8th murder of ex-Beatle John Lennon in New York City. The killer, Mark David Chapman, had lived for the past three years in Honolulu and bought the gun he used to shoot Lennon at a Young Street gun shop.

The average cost of a single-family home on O'ahu is now about $150,000, a sum that would have been considered outrageous even a few years ago.

The first nine trustees for the newly created Office of Hawaiian Affairs are elected. The election is seen as a significant step toward giving native Hawaiians more of a say in determining their affairs. Another success for native Hawaiians is the approval of a bill introduced by President Carter to establish the Native Hawaiian Claims Commission.

January 5—A "once-in-a-hundred-years" storm socks the Islands, leaving seven people dead and millions of dollars of damage in its wake.

April 1—Gov. George Ariyoshi admits that Hawai'i, with a de facto population of over 1 million, is growing too fast.

September 20—Former State Budget Director Eileen Anderson, a relative political newcomer, wrests away Honolulu Mayor Frank Fasi's long and powerful hold on City Hall in the Democratic primary election. That victory, with the backing of Gov. Ariyoshi and an experienced campaign team, propels her to an easy win in the general election. With the victory, Anderson becomes Honolulu's first woman mayor.

December—The U.S. Department of Transportation approves the state's environmental impact study of the proposed H-3 trans-Ko'olau freeway, paving the way for construction. However, environmentalists vow to continue their opposition of the project.

1981

The Alexander Young Hotel, an eighty-year-old landmark in downtown Honolulu, is finally demolished after several attempts to save it through the courts.

Mid Pacific Airlines enters the inter-island flight scene, but suffers from concerted attempts by the two other existing local airlines to prevent the newcomer from gaining a market foothold.

The sugar industry continues its decline. As Congress passes a price-support bill that leaves growers unhappy, and Amfac hints at phasing out its Waipahu sugar operations, the debate continues over how much effort should be put into saving the Islands' sugar industry.

Demonstrations at the judiciary buildings and the State Capitol draw thousands of people protesting an innocent verdict handed down to a group of O'ahu boys charged with gang raping a dental student from Finland. Legislators are sufficiently moved by this spontaneous display of public anger to amend the state rape law to clarify that a woman does not need to resist for a rape to occur.

The University of Hawai'i is the subject of a scathing report by the legislative auditor's office, which looked at its organization, planning, and personnel policies. The report proves to be useful ammunition for long-time critics of the UH administration, who use the criticisms to block three of the governor's seven appointments to the Board of Regents. In September, UH President Fujio Matsuda fires Mānoa Chancellor Durward Long,

saying that henceforth he will only be a history professor. The action provokes Long to threaten to reveal publicly the inner workings of the institution. Three weeks later Matsuda creates a new vice-presidency position for Long, which some people claim is done to keep Long quiet.

December 5—Two days before the fortieth anniversary of the attack on Pearl Harbor, eleven skydivers die when their plane crashes into shallow harbor waters close to the USS *Arizona* Memorial.

1982

Hawaiian activists such as Haunani Kay-Trask decry the loss of Hawaiian values and debate how traditional ways can be preserved given the pressures of modern life.

The federal government approves designs for the long-controversial H-3 freeway, a 10-mile stretch that will bore through the Ko'olaus and past a facility emitting potentially hazardous radio waves.

George Ariyoshi is elected to his third term as governor after spending $2.5 million to fend off opponents Jean King in the primary and Senator D.G. "Andy" Anderson and former Mayor Frank Fasi in the general election. The GOP reaches a nadir in party history with only thirteen Republican legislators surviving the election.

State leadership faces a public confidence problem after the pesticide heptachlor, federally banned as a carcinogen, is found to have contaminated milk products on the Islands for more than a year and a half, and traces are found in mother's milk. Millions of dollars are lost as dairies are closed and new cows are brought in from the mainland. Litigation is heavy, and Health Department Director George Yuen resigns in the middle of the crisis. Milk is recalled again in December, this time due to the discovery of an overdose of antibiotics.

April—The military carries out bombing target practice on the island of Kaho'olawe as part of the five-nation RIMPAC naval exercises. Harry Kunihi Mitchell, of Protect Kaho'olawe and Greenpeace, paddles to the island to protest the exercises, following the path of his son, Kimo, who disappeared on a similar surfboard voyage five years earlier.

September—Arguments over aboriginal and indigenous rights stall progress on determining what Hawaiians are owed from lands lost during the 1893 overthrow of the monarchy. The federal Native Hawaiian Study Commission, appointed in 1980 to examine the "culture, needs and concerns" of Hawaiians, later reports that Hawaiians have no legal claim to lost lands under present law.

November 23—Hurricane 'Iwa strikes O'ahu, Ni'ihau, and Kaua'i with winds as high as 117 miles an hour, causing an estimated $234 million in damage (mainly on Kaua'i). This was the most destructive storm ever to hit Hawai'i.

December 19—The University of Hawai'i Rainbow Wahines come back from a two-game deficit to beat two-time defending champion USC and claim the national title.

December 23—Chaminade University defies the odds to defeat the number-one-ranked University of Virginia college basketball team.

1983

The official population of Hawai'i reaches 1,083,000. The Island's ethnic distribution breaks down to 24.5 percent Caucasian, 23.2 percent Japanese, 11.3 percent Filipino, and 20.0 percent Hawaiian and part-Hawaiian.

A multimillion-dollar state budget surplus evaporates just before Governor Ariyoshi begins his third term. He orders all state agencies, as well as semi-public agencies, to trim their budgets.

Scores of brushfires burn along the dry Wai'anae coast during the summer. Investigators say they are set by arsonists who apparently toss road flares from passing cars. Firefighters blame an electric golf cart for a $1 million fire at the Waialae Country Club that destroys a caddie shack holding 738 sets of members' golf clubs.

January 3—A flank eruption on the East Rift Zone of Kīlauea Volcano at Nāpau Crater sends up 250-foot fountains of lava. The activity moves to Pu'u 'Ō'ō Vent in June of 1983 and sends lava fountains 1,400 feet high. Lava flows eventually reach the Royal Gardens subdivision and bury or burn sixteen homes.

April 1—The family of Radio KSSK station owner Cecil Heftel apologizes for the station's elaborate April Fool's joke, which brings hundreds of people to Waikīkī to see a non-existent parade supposedly starring Tom Selleck.

July—One police officer resigns and three others are suspended in connection with an investigation of cocaine use and distribution within the police department. The investigation targets ten to twelve Kāne'ohe police officers.

July 13—An 'Ewa cane fire short-circuits power lines near the Kahe Power Plant, plunging O'ahu into an unprecedented mass power outage. When pumps also fail, city officials divert raw sewage into the Ala Wai Canal and Lake Wilson.

August—In one of Hawai'i's most famous corporate scandals, the investment firm of Bishop, Baldwin, Rewald, Dillingham and Wong suffers financial collapse due to the manipulations of Ron Rewald, who had deceived investors by claiming prestigious local connections and great financial success. He was known for his lavish parties and sponsorship of polo matches. As a result of Rewald's activities, 418 investors lose about $20 million. In 1985 Rewald is convicted of ninety-four counts of tax evasion, perjury, and fraud, and sentenced to eighteen years in federal prison. He is released in 1995 due to a back injury.

September 21—On Moloka'i, police arrest a handful of people protesting the bulldozing of the Hale Mohalu Hansens's disease treatment center, located in Pearl City, O'ahu, which was closed in 1978. Bulldozers take only a few minutes to level the ramshackle wooden and tin structures that were once homes for the afflicted.

November—A federal appeals court orders the state to stop condemning property under the Land Reform Act, which was passed to break up large landholdings.

November—In the first strike in the University of Hawai'i's history, faculty members stage a walkout that ends after two days.

November 13—An earthquake measuring 6.7 on the Richter scale hits the Islands, causing numerous injuries.

December—The University of Hawaiʻi Rainbow Wahine women's volleyball team defeats UCLA in three straight games to claim the second of its back-to-back NCAA championships.

1985

Businessman David H. Murdock, chief executive of the "Big Five" company Castle & Cooke, purchases 98 percent of the island of Lānaʻi. He ends pineapple production on Lānaʻi and begins constructing two new luxury resorts as well as expensive townhouses.

The annual visitor count in the Hawaiian Islands tops 5 million.

What once seemed like never-ending work on the Kūhiō Avenue road-widening project finally ends, allowing traffic to flow smoothly in Waikīkī.

January 25—Big Island native Ellison Onizuka travels to space in the space shuttle.

1986

When students build a shantytown to protest the University of Hawaiʻi's South African investments, the publicity moves the UH Board of Regents to divest.

Reeling over public criticism of his staff, Superintendent Francis Hatanaka quits his job rather than wait for the school board to issue a "report card."

January 28—Ellison Onizuka, the first Hawaiʻi-born astronaut and the first American of Japanese ancestry to fly in space, dies with the crew of the space shuttle Challenger as it explodes after takeoff from Florida's Kennedy Space Center.

February 25—Ousted Philippines dictator Ferdinand Marcos arrives in exile aboard a U.S. Air Force transport plane with his wife, Imelda, and eighty-nine relatives, friends, and assistants, as well as $8 million in cash and jewels. Marcos lives lavishly for the next three and a half years before succumbing to heart and kidney problems. He passes away on September 28, 1989, at St. Francis Medical Center.

May 21—Mary Kawena Pukui, one of Hawaiʻi's most revered scholars of Hawaiian culture, passes away at the age of ninety-one.

July 3—Waipahu student Hue Cao, 12, flies to New York to read her essay "What the Statue of Liberty Means to Me" as 1.5 billion people watch on television.

September 21—John D. Waiheʻe sweeps past Cecil Heftel to an upset win in the Democratic primary for governor, and later becomes the first person of Hawaiian ancestry to be elected governor of Hawaiʻi when he defeats Republican D.G. "Andy" Anderson. Another notable political "first" includes Pat Saiki's becoming the first Republican from Hawaiʻi elected to the U.S. House. The sports world also sees important firsts involving Hawaiʻi athletes: Al Noga, a University of Hawaiʻi defensive tackle, becomes the first Hawaiʻi player voted to the AP All-American first team, and Sid Fernandez becomes the first Hawaiʻi baseball player to pitch in a World Series.

October 1—The legal drinking age increases from eighteen to twenty-one years of age.

December 7—Officials break ground for West Beach, a development near Barbers Point billed as Oʻahu's "Second City."

1987

"Hoʻolako 1987," the Year of the Hawaiian, is celebrated to honor Hawaiian culture.

February 21—The "Quiksilver in Memory of Eddie Aikau" surf contest is held, matching the world's best big wave surfers against each other. The first "Eddie" is won by Clyde Aikau, the brother of Eddie Aikau.

May 23—The Polynesian voyaging canoe Hōkūleʻa completes a two-year "voyage of discovery" to demonstrate native navigational methods.

December 31—A devastating storm on New Year's Eve causes widespread damage on Hawaiʻi Island and Oʻahu.

1988

May 1—The *Magnum PI* television series, starring Tom Selleck and filmed in Hawaiʻi, ends after eight seasons.

Tourism now contributes to 32 percent of the state's economy, up from 3 percent in the 1950s.

April 28—Aloha Airlines Flight 243 is en route from Hilo to Honolulu when a large chunk of the jet's roof and walls are suddenly torn from the plane's cabin. A flight attendant standing at seat row 5 disappears through the hole in the left side of the fuselage. Another flight attendant is hit in the head by the windstorm of debris and suffers head lacerations and a concussion. The $5 million Aloha Airlines Boeing 737 airplane sustains major damage and has to be dismantled and sold for parts and scrap.

1989

Foreign investment in Hawaiʻi becomes a hot business issue as billions of dollars pour into the state from overseas. Japanese businesses dominate the investment scene, primarily in real estate, with solid representation also from Australia, New Zealand, Hong Kong, and Indonesia. The tsunami of investment invigorates Hawaiʻi's economy, but it also prompts strong feelings about economic and social issues. In a poll, 60 percent of Hawaiʻi residents claim to be somewhat or strongly opposed to Japanese investment, while 37 percent take the opposite view.

Visa fraud indictments are handed down to several well-to-do Japanese investors after state officials determine that they failed to disclose past criminal records.

Hawaiʻi's recent tourism boom sees visitor spending increase to $10.4 billion for the year. Although this is 26 percent higher than a decade ago, the growth depends on a "fragile" industry. Many economic experts consider this dependency dangerously high.

February 24—Shortly after taking off from Honolulu International Airport, a United Airlines 747 flying to Sydney, Australia, experiences an electrical short that causes a cargo door to open, triggering an explosive decompression and loss of power in two engines. Nine passengers are sucked out of the plane over the Pacific Ocean and never recovered. The plane returns to Honolulu and lands safely.

1990

Officials at the prominent Center Art Galleries are convicted of fraud in a multimillion-dollar swindle involving reproductions of works by Salvador Dali. The defense puts up superstar witnesses Red Skelton and Tony Curtis, both of whom credit the galleries for their own successes as painters.

January 17—Operation Desert Storm begins in the Persian Gulf in response to Iraq's invasion of Kuwait on August 2, 1989. The war eventually requires the services of more than 7,000 troops based in Kāneʻohe before Iraq accepts United Nations conditions and resolutions on April 7, 1990.

April-October—Lava flows from Kīlauea Volcano on Hawaiʻi Island destroy numerous homes in and around Kalapana Gardens, as well as Walter Yamaguchi's Kalapana Store and the Mauna Kea Congregational Church. By the end of 1990 the destruction totals 181 homes, and the famous black sand beach on crescent-shaped Kaimū Bay has filled with lava. The volcano, which has erupted continuously since 1983, still pumps hot ooze.

May 16—Daniel Akaka becomes the first U.S. Senator of Native Hawaiian ancestry.

June—The Army, despite objections from environmentalists and community groups, begins testing its chemical weapons incinerator at Johnston Island, 825 miles southwest of Hawaiʻi. In November, U.S. chemical arms begin arriving on the island from West Germany.

November 6—Governor John Waiheʻe fends off an election-year challenge by State Rep. Fred Hemmings. The deaths of U.S. Sen. Spark Matsunaga and Big Island Mayor Bernard Akana kick off a scramble for their seats, with a similar situation occurring when two congressional seats are vacated by Reps. Daniel Akaka and Pat Saiki. President Bush is brought in to help campaign for Rep. Saiki while Senator Ted Kennedy steps up to bat for Rep. Akaka, who eventually wins the senatorial election.

1991

June—The state government unveils

plans to build villages for homeless people around Oʻahu. In some communities, however, opposition to these villages results in the plans being dropped.

August—Twelve Island chefs form Hawaiʻi Regional Cuisine, Inc. to promote the new world-class cuisine. Hawaiʻi Regional cuisine features fresh local fish and vegetables as well as exotic Island fruits and utilizes culinary techniques from both the Eastern and Western traditions.

November 14—City Council approves a $1.7 billion, 15.6-mile rail transit system from Wahiawa to the University of Hawaiʻi at Mānoa. Transit foes view the proposal as an example of government waste and proof of politicians' disdain of local people's wishes. Councilman Andy Mirikitani, who casts the decisive vote for the project, frames the decision in terms of "tough choices" and a positive "legacy we leave for future generations."

1992

April 14—The Keck Telescope, the largest optical-infrared telescope in the world, becomes operable atop Mauna Kea Volcano. In 1996 the Keck II becomes operable, and in March of 2001, the light-gathering powers of the two powerful Keck telescopes are combined.

September 11—Hurricane ʻIniki makes a direct hit on Kauaʻi. The hurricane damages 14,000 homes, causes $1.8 billion in damage, and shuts down 90 percent of the island's vacation accommodations. The hurricane, one of the costliest natural disasters in U.S. history, leads many insurance companies to place a moratorium on new homeowners' policies.

September 22—A City Council committee votes five to four to kill Honolulu's rail-transit system. Defeated is a bill that would have increased the general excise tax from 4 percent to 4.5 percent to help pay for the $1.7 billion project. Councilwoman Rene Mansho, who casts the key vote against the project, says there are still too many unanswered questions.

November—Officials launch shark hunts off Oʻahu after Aaron Romento is killed by sharks off Keaʻau Beach, Rick

Gruzinsky is attacked off Laniākea, and Bryan Adona vanishes at Leftovers, near Waimea Bay, and his board is found half-eaten.

November 4—A large area around the Hawaiian Islands is designated as the Hawaiian Islands Humpback Whale National Marine Sanctuary. Governor Benjamin Cayetano approves the sanctuary on June 5, 1997.

December—Ground is broken on the $32.24 million Special Events Arena, which in 1998 is renamed the Stan Sheriff Center.

1993

Democratic Hawaiʻi Senator Richard Matsuura heads a special Senate committee that uncovers numerous questionable practices by state officials within his own party. The investigation, which focuses on how the Waiheʻe administration buys goods and services, and what real estate investments are made or considered by the State Employees' Retirement System, eventually leads to the resignation of Waiheʻe administration Budget Director Yukio Takemoto.

January 17—ʻOnipaʻa (stand fast) ceremonies are held at ʻIolani Palace on the one-hundredth anniversary of the 1893 overthrow of the Hawaiian monarchy. The ceremonies draw thousands who mourn the events of the past and call for a restoration of native sovereignty. A rallying point for Hawaiian sovereignty groups is the island of Kahoʻolawe, which the federal government has agreed to hand over to the state, and later to a sovereign, native Hawaiian entity, after having used it for fifty years in military bombing exercises. Proponents of Hawaiian sovereignty are also aided by the legislature's establishment of the Hawaiian Sovereignty Advisory Commission, which will draft proposals to create a governing framework for a new Hawaiian nation.

May 5—The national spotlight lands on Hawaiʻi as the State Supreme Court rules in favor of same-sex marriage, making it possible for Hawaiʻi to become the first U.S. state to allow gay marriages. Rep. Terrance Tom, chairman of the State House Judiciary Commission, hears heated arguments from hundreds

of people who testified at legislative hearings on same-sex marriage around the state.

July 11-14—President Bill Clinton pays a three-day visit to Hawaiʻi following a summit in Japan and a visit to South Korea. During his stay he meets the press on the beach at Waikīkī, an "event" paid for by local Democrats and Friends of Clinton. Due to flooding in the Midwest, however, he cuts his Hawaiʻi visit short.

November 23—Acknowledging the 100th anniversary of the illegal overthrow of the Kingdom of Hawaiʻi, United States President Bill Clinton signs Public Law 103-150, an apology to native Hawaiians on behalf of the United States, written as a Joint Resolution of Congress.

December 3—In a special legislative session, lawmakers choose the Aloha Motors site, just outside Waikīkī, for a convention center. The state buys the 9.6-acre site from developer Sukarman Sukamto for $136 million.

1994

February 12—Two kaʻai—woven burial baskets believed to contain the bones of 15th century Hawaiian chiefs—are discovered missing from the Bishop Museum.

May 7—In a ceremony held on Maui, the federal government hands over to the state the island of Kahoʻolawe, which has been used for military bombing target practice for fifty years. Bombing was halted in 1990 after more than two decades of intense local opposition.

June—The state government offers the Independent Nation of Hawaiʻi, a Hawaiian sovereignty group that seeks to gain control of lands held by the state since Queen Liliʻuokalani's overthrow, a lease on 69 acres of Waimanalo land. The agreement ends a fifteen-month occupation of Makapuʻu and Kaupo beach parks on Oʻahu.

August 20—During a weekend Circus International performance at Blaisdell Arena, thousands of Islanders witness the televised police killing of a circus elephant named Tyke after the 9000-pound animal fatally mauls her trainer, Allen Campbell, and efforts to calm or corner her fail.

November—Aloha Tower Marketplace is built in Honolulu on Piers 8, 9, 10, and 11.

November 9—Bucking the trend elsewhere in the United States, Democrats maintain an overwhelming majority in Hawaiʻi's Legislature and head the state administration. In Hawaiʻi's gubernatorial race, former lieutenant governor Ben Cayetano defeats Republican Pat Saiki and Best Party candidate Frank Fasi, becoming the first U.S. governor of Filipino ancestry. Mazie Hirono becomes lieutenant governor, and, in a hint of things to come, Maui's Republican mayor, Linda Crockett Lingle, wins a second term. Cayetano, who had been lieutenant governor under John D. Waiheʻe, serves as governor until 2002.

1995

June 4—Pope John Paul II beatifies Hawaiian hero Father Damien DeVeuster in Brussels, Belgium, bringing the priest one step closer to sainthood. Following the ceremony, a reliquary holding Damien's right hand is brought back to Hawaiʻi for reinterment. Father Damien ministered to leprosy (Hansen's disease) patients at Kalaupapa, Molokaʻi, from 1873 until he died in 1889.

September 2—The fiftieth anniversary of VJ Day, held to commemorate the end of World War II, is highlighted by President Clinton's visit. Clinton takes part in various ceremonies marking the anniversary, and old enemies shake hands as Japanese and American war veterans seek to heal the lingering trauma of war. War veterans from both sides of the former conflict fill hotels in Waikīkī and visit the sights of peacetime Hawaiʻi.

1996

October 18—The First Hawaiian Center is dedicated in downtown Honolulu, becoming Hawaiʻi's tallest building.

November 5—President Bill Clinton stages a strong political comeback, overcoming charges of irrelevancy in the wake of a Republican congressional sweep two years earlier, to defeat Republican presidential nominee Bob Dole. Clinton is aided by a continuing strong economy and the fact that the country remains at peace. Despite his victory, various ethical questions and scandals persist into his second term as president.

November 6—Several powerful state lawmakers are unseated in elections as voters vent their wrath over the legislature's failure to reach agreement on auto insurance reform and same-sex marriage. Jeremy Harris wins the Honolulu mayoral race while Circuit Judge Kevin Chang garners national attention when he rules that the state has failed to demonstrate a compelling interest in banning same-sex marriage.

1997

May 16—Brook Lee, who is from Pearl City and was named Miss USA in February, is crowned Miss Universe.

June 26—Renowned Hawaiian musician Israel Ka'ano'i Kamakawiwo'ole passes away at age thirty-eight due to respiratory failure. As Hawai'i's most popular entertainer and singer, "Bruddah Iz" won numerous Nā Hōkū Hanohano awards and became famous worldwide. Thousands memorialize him at the State Capitol Rotunda.

July 8—Gay couples, who are not legally entitled to marry, are extended some of the benefits given to married people when the state's first-in-the-nation reciprocal benefits law goes into effect. The law is a compromise based on a 1993 Hawai'i Supreme Court ruling that found it unconstitutional to deny marriage licenses to same-sex couples.

August 7—Police, sheriffs, and state workers haul away the belongings of families camped near Mokuleia Beach Park.

August 9—A *Star-Bulletin* article titled "Broken Trust," written by prominent community members, including a former Kamehameha Schools principal, calls for Bishop Estate reforms. Three days later, in a push for immediate action, the governor asks State Attorney General Margery Bronster to investigate the matter. The investigation eventually leads to the removal of trustees. Since then, historic changes have been made in the governance of the 114-year-old trust.

August 11—Lava breaches the walls of the Big Island's 800-year-old Waha'ula

Heiau, consuming one of the most sacred of Hawaiian temples.

August 30—After community groups stage protests, the military cancels plans to conduct a landing exercise at Makua Beach.

October 14—Three-year-old Alana Dung passes away after a long battle against leukemia. Her battle touches thousands of people and spurs the community in the cause for bone marrow donation.

October 31—A city employee is arrested on theft and bribery charges in the Ewa Villages relocation scandal. Fourteen people are eventually arrested, including two City Housing Department employees. The criminal probe focused on the suspects' use of their city positions to have friends relocate 'Ewa Village tenants at exorbitant prices.

December 12—Opening ceremonies are held for the H-3 "Trans-Ko'olau" freeway connecting Honolulu to Kailua and Kāne'ohe on O'ahu's Windward side. The 16.1-mile freeway took thirty years to complete due to legal battles, design changes, environmental concerns, and controversies about intruding on the culturally significant Hālawa and Ha'ikū valleys. The $1.3 billion cost of the freeway, which is eighteen times the original price-tag, makes it the most expensive public works project in the state's history, with 26 bridges, 2 long viaducts, and 2 sets of tunnels 4,890 feet long in the Kāne'ohe-bound direction and 5,165 feet in the Hālawa-bound direction.

December 20—Hawai'i Supreme Court justices say they will no longer appoint Bishop Estate trustees.

1998

January 2—Legendary surfer Rell Kapolioka'ehukai Sunn, known as the "Queen of Mākaha," passes away due to breast cancer. Three thousand people attend her funeral at Mākaha.

April 15—City prosecutors expand their investigation into alleged fraud at the Ewa Villages project. Although the original probe involved the use of relocation money, prosecutors now look at the city's Housing Department Property Management branch. In May, an

O'ahu grand jury indicts eight people in the scheme.

June 11—The Hawai'i Convention Center opens in Honolulu.

July—In a genetic-engineering breakthrough, University of Hawai'i postdoctoral student Teruhiko Wakayama develops a new cloning technique that produces, from adult cells, three generations of genetically identical cloned mice (e.g., a clone of a clone of a clone).

July 16—The Friends of 'Iolani Palace board struggles with a conflict between board president Abigail Kawananakoa and palace director Jim Bartels. The dispute arises when Kawananakoa sits on and possibly damages a royal throne. This leads to Bartels' resignation. Kawananakoa is later removed as board president.

September 10—Attorney General Bronster calls for the permanent removal of Bishop Estate trustees Henry Peters, Richard "Dickie" Wong, and Lokelani Lindsey. In October the estate agrees to implement a new management system headed by a chief executive officer, and in November Henry Peters is indicted by an O'ahu grand jury on one count of theft.

November 3—Hawai'i's general election voters re-elect Ben Cayetano governor and overwhelmingly approve a constitutional amendment to allow the legislature to ban same-sex marriage.

December 10—June Jones is hired as UH head football coach less than two weeks after Fred vonAppen is fired.

December 19—The Vatican clarifies rules affecting hula performed during church services, saying "sacred gestures" are permitted as a form of worship but dancing as entertainment is inappropriate.

1999

The controversy involving Kamehameha Schools Bishop Estate comes to a climax after nearly three years, as all five trustees resign amidst charges of mismanagement of the estate's $6 billion trust, taking excessive compensation, and neglect of the estate's core mission to educate native Hawaiians.

January 29—The 58,000-ton U.S.S. *Missouri* battleship opens as a tourist attraction at Pearl Harbor.

February 12—The Senate acquits President Clinton of perjury and obstruction of justice.

February 24—The FBI probes a sinister anthrax-hoax after an Ala Moana office worker opens a suspicious letter.

April 28—An uproar ensues after the state Senate rejects the reconfirmations of Attorney General Margery Bronster and Budget Director Earl Anzai, with Gov. Ben Cayetano suggesting that Bronster's investigation into Bishop Estate is a contributing factor in the decision. Two months later Cayetano selects Anzai as his new attorney general.

May 9 (Mother's Day)—A hike turns into a nightmare when a landslide at a popular O'ahu waterfall and swimming hole in Sacred Falls State Park kills three men, four women, and a seven-year-old girl who dies in the arms of her would-be rescuers. Falling debris and boulders injure fifty others.

October 8—The *Hōkūle'a* nears the completion of its voyage to retrace Polynesian migration routes when it lands in Rapa Nui. The *Hōkūle'a* has now sailed each of the major Polynesian migration routes and docked at each corner of the Polynesian triangle: Hawai'i, New Zealand, and Rap Nui. The *Hōkūle'a* returns to Hawai'i in March of 2000 to celebrate twenty-five years of seafaring.

November 2—The worst mass murder in Hawai'i's history occurs when O'ahu Xerox worker Bryan Uyesugi shoots seven co-workers. Uyesugi surrenders to police after a manhunt ends in a six-hour standoff at the Hawai'i Nature Park in Makiki.

December—As the year 2000 approaches, with its shadow of a possible Y2K computer bug looming, merchants in Hawai'i report brisk sales of fireworks for what even Gov. Ben Cayetano says he hopes will be the last year they can be set off legally.

2000

February 23—In the legal case *Rice vs. Cayetano,* the U.S. Supreme Court rules seven to two that Hawaiians-only voting in elections for trustees of the Office of Hawaiian Affairs (OHA) violates the Fifteenth Amendment's ban on race-based voting restrictions. The court ruling is the result of a lawsuit against the state by Hawai'i Island rancher Harold "Freddy" Rice, a fifth-generation kama'āina (born in Hawai'i) who was barred from voting in an OHA election.

July 20—U.S. Senator Daniel Akaka introduces the Native Hawaiian Reorganization Act, known as the Akaka Bill, to provide federal recognition to native Hawaiians and protect federal funding of Hawaiian entitlements that were jeopardized by the recent U.S. Supreme Court decision in *Rice v. Cayetano*. The House of Representatives passes the Akaka Bill on October 24, 2007.

December 8—President Clinton proclaims a Coral Reef Ecosystem Reserve that covers more than 1,200 miles in the Northwestern Hawaiian Islands.

2001

January 20—George W. Bush becomes the forty-third President of the United States.

February 9—The fast-attack submarine USS *Greeneville* is engaged in a rapid-ascent surfacing drill nine miles off Pearl Harbor when it crashes into the *Ehime Maru*, a fishing boat on a training expedition with students from southwestern Japan's Uwajima Fisheries High School aboard. The submarine rips open the trawler's bulkheads and fuel tanks, killing nine of the *Ehime Maru*'s crew members and sinking the ship. In 2003, the Navy pays $13 million to the families of the victims.

March 12—Engineers and scientists at the Keck telescopes atop Mauna Kea succeed in combining the light-gathering powers of the two 10-meter Keck telescopes, forming the world's largest optical interferometer. In 2002 they break the record for sighting the most distant objects ever seen by viewing a galaxy estimated to be 15.5 billion light years away.

March 15—The *Honolulu Star Bulletin* publishes its first edition under the ownership of Canadian publisher David Black. The newspaper's sale ends a

protracted legal battle with Honolulu Advertiser parent Gannett Co. and starts the first head-to-head newspaper competition in Honolulu in nearly forty years.

April 5—Following a collapse in labor contract negotiations, public education in Hawai'i is shut down by the state's first combined upper and lower education strikes involving 3,000 University of Hawai'i faculty and 10,000 public school teachers.

May 22—Disney stages a $5 million movie premiere-extravaganza for the movie *Pearl Harbor* on the flight deck of the U.S.S. *John C. Stennis* aircraft carrier in Pearl Harbor. Some Pearl Harbor survivors who attend the showing return in December for ceremonies marking the sixtieth anniversary of the attack that plunged the United States into World War II.

July 8—O'ahu residents band together to fight the island's shrieking coqui frog invasion.

September 11—Terrorists hijack four passenger jets, flying two into the World Trade Center towers in New York, crashing one into the Pentagon building in Arlington, Virginia, and another in a Pennsylvania field. The attacks kill nearly 3,000 Americans, including Hawai'i natives Maile Hale, Heather Ho, Richard Lee, and Patricia Pitchford, and Hawai'i residents Christine Snyder and Georgine Corrigan, who were both aboard the jet that crashed in Pennsylvania. Immediately after the attack, tourism drops more than 30 percent.

November 23—The day after Thanksgiving, department store chain Liberty House, a retailing institution headquartered in Hawai'i for more than a century, opens its doors as Macy's, which bought the company earlier in the year.

2002

May 2—Dog lovers the world over are captivated by the plight of Hok Get, a two-year-old terrier rescued by a Coast Guard tugboat. The wayward dog was left aboard a burned-out tanker and survived on rainwater and rats for nearly a month. She is welcomed to Honolulu by a media frenzy and the state's mandatory 120-day pet quarantine.

May 30—Mayor Jeremy Harris, the presumed front-runner for the Democratic gubernatorial nomination, drops a political bombshell when he announces he will drop out of the race. His decision negates the need for a mayoral race that already has a field of potential candidates, including Lt. Governor Mazie Hirono, who immediately jumps back into the gubernatorial race. Harris' 2000 mayoral campaign continues to be the subject of a criminal investigation involving city contractors.

September 23—Hawai'i's gubernatorial race takes shape as Democrat Mazie Hirono and Republican Linda Lingle court voters.

September 28—U.S. Rep. Patsy Mink, who in 1964 became the first Asian-American woman elected to the U.S. Congress, passes away, leaving behind not only a legacy of unabashed liberalism but also a political free-for-all for her office. The longtime Democrat is eulogized for her fight for civil rights for women and minorities.

November 5—Linda Lingle, the former mayor of Maui County, is elected governor of the state of Hawai'i while Duke Aiona wins the Lieutenant Governor election. Lingle's campaign theme promises "A New Beginning" and makes a major issue of political corruption among Democrats. Lingle becomes the state's first woman governor and the first Republican governor in forty years. The contest against Lt. Gov. Mazie Hirono represented the nation's second matchup of two women in a gubernatorial election.

2003

Federal spending in the state of Hawai'i totals $11.27 billion, including $4.84 billion in defense spending. Compared to other states, Hawai'i ranks sixth in federal spending, and second among all states in per-capita defense spending.

February 2—Hawai'i mourns the loss of seven astronauts after the space shuttle *Columbia* breaks apart.

2004

January 13—The Vatican's Congregation for the Causes of Saints affirms Mother Marianne's "heroic virtue,"

which is a step toward canonization and sainthood.

April 7—Willis McInnis, 57, of Napili, dies after a shark mangles his leg about two hundred yards offshore in Kahana, Maui. His death is the fourth in the Isles attributed to sharks since 1991. Six months later a diver survives after being bitten by a 12-foot shark off eastern Moloka'i.

June 15—The University of Hawai'i Board of Regents fires UH president Evan Dobelle "for cause," which the contract defines as corruption, mental illness, or criminal behavior. The highly controversial decision tarnishes the university, the board, and Dobelle. On July 29, after arbitration, the Regents rescind their decision. Dobelle is given a resignation severance worth $3.2 million and absolved of any wrongdoing. In October Dobelle shows his resilience by being named president of the New England Board of Higher Education.

June 29—The biennial Rim of the Pacific (RIMPAC) naval exercises take place in Hawaiian waters, lasting until July 27. The exercises include more than 35 ships, 90 aircraft, 7 submarines and 11,000 soldiers, airmen, sailors, Marines, and Coast Guard.

August 18—Island icon Hiram Fong, who became the first elected Asian-American U.S. Senator in 1959, passes away at the age of 97.

October 30—Mānoa Stream, bulging with rainwater, floods more than 190 homes and businesses, an elementary school, and several buildings on the University of Hawai'i campus, where it destroys books, maps, manuscripts, and irreplaceable historic documents at UH, and causes up to $100 million in damage.

November 2—Mufi Hannemann is elected mayor of Honolulu with a margin of victory of only about 1300 votes. According to media polls, mayoral candidate Duke Bainum had all the momentum going into the election. Hannemann becomes Honolulu's twelfth mayor and the first of Samoan ancestry.

December—The annual visitor count for the Hawaiian Islands is 6,908,173, an 8.3 percent increase over 2003, just shy of the record 6.95 million who visited in 2000. Visitor expenditures total $10.3 billion, an all-time high along with total visitor days (62.8 million).

2005

January 26—A Marine Corps helicopter crashes during a sandstorm in western Iraq, killing thirty-one U.S. servicemen including twenty-six Kāneʻohe Marines and a Pearl Harbor sailor. The crash is the single deadliest event since the beginning of the war in March of 2003.

August 2—A panel of the 9th U.S. Circuit of Appeals rules two to one that Kamehameha Schools' 117-year-old policy of restricting admission to native Hawaiians is "unlawful race discrimination." Kamehameha Schools petitions for a rehearing, and five days later more than 10,000 supporters rally against a ruling to disallow the Hawaiians-first admission policy.

October 5—Fifteen-year-old golfing phenomenon Michelle Wie declares that she is turning professional and has signed endorsement deals with Nike and Sony worth up to $10 million a year, making her the world's highest-paid female golfer and the third highest-paid female in any sport.

December 27—Eddie Ayau, leader of the Hui Malama I Nā Kūpuna O Hawaiʻi Nei group, is sentenced to jail for refusing to disclose where eighty-three rare Hawaiian artifacts, recently housed at the Bishop Museum, have been reburied in caves on the Big Island. The saga leaves the Hawaiian community deeply divided.

2006

January—U.S. Rep. Ed Case challenges longtime U.S. Sen. Daniel Akaka for his seat in Congress, shocking his Democratic party and setting the stage for a dramatic year in Hawaiʻi politics. Defending his decision to run, Case says the state must prepare for a new generation of leaders in Congress. His opponents vilify him for stepping out of line. Supported by the party's major players, Akaka wins the Democratic primary with 54 percent of the vote to Case's 45 percent. Akaka claims that Case's challenge has united the party but it has also shown the strains. In the general election Akaka easily defeats Republican State Rep. Cynthia Thielen.

March 14—When Kauaʻi's Ka Loko dam breaks, the force of the flowing waters destroys ten homes, damages dozens of others, and kills seven people. The break leads to a statewide inspection of all dams and opens a potentially lengthy legal battle to establish responsibility.

April 1—Torrential rain pounds Oʻahu, wreaking havoc on homes, businesses, and streets.

May 31—Donald Trump will develop a $350 million luxury condo-hotel in Waikīkī.

June 8—The Akaka Bill falls four votes short of breaking a filibuster, preventing it from going to the Senate for a vote. Senator Akaka reintroduces the bill on January 17, 2007.

June 15—President Bush designates the Northwestern Hawaiian Islands Marine National Monument by signing Presidential Proclamation 8031. The newly declared monument extends 1,400 miles to the northwest of Kauaʻi, and includes many small islands, islets, reefs, and atolls that are home to 14 million seabirds as well as land birds, native fish, sea turtles, and monk seals.

October 15—A pair of early-morning earthquakes off the Big Island rattles much of Hawaiʻi. The shaking caused by the magnitude 6.7 and 6.0 quakes results in damage to roads, bridges, port facilities, churches, hotels, and homes. Most of Oʻahu is without power for hours, and damages on the Big Island are expected to top $100 million. Fortunately, no one dies.

November 21—Honolulu police officer Steve Favela suffers multiple injuries after crashing his motorcycle while escorting President Bush at Hickam Air Force Base. He dies five days later, becoming the sixth Honolulu officer to die in the line of duty since July 1995. "Officer Favela risked his life every day to protect the people of his community. In this time of great sadness, we give thanks for his life of service," President Bush said in a statement issued by the White House.

December 22—A historic City Council vote approves a mass transit system the largest transit system ever approved in the state with an estimated price tag of nearly $5 billion. Many residents wonder if the city can afford to pay for the proposed 28-mile route and if enough people will use it.

2007

March 8—On Kauaʻi, a Heli USA tour helicopter plunges into the grass by the Princeville Airport runway, killing the pilot and three passengers and critically injuring three others. Four days later the Garden Isle witnesses a second fatal helicopter crash when an Inter-Island helicopter loses its tail rotor and plummets to the ground in Hāʻena. One passenger is killed while the pilot and three others are injured.

April 14—Don Ho, the popular entertainer whose career spanned half a century and whose name was synonymous with Hawaiʻi, passes away at age seventy-six. Three weeks later the state mourns his death as thousands flock to Waikīkī for a service honoring the man who sang "I'll Remember You."

August—Kauaʻi and Maui opponents of the Superferry, a massive catamaran-style transport boat, use civil disobedience and the courts to stop the ship from moving hundreds of passengers and their cars between islands. Months later, following a special session of the State Legislature, the Superferry is back in business.

August 22—Ten Schofield Barracks soldiers are among fourteen killed in a Black Hawk helicopter crash in northern Iraq. Forty-one soldiers did not return home with the roughly 7000 25th Infantry Division soldiers who completed a fifteen-month deployment to Iraq in the fall.

November 24—The University of Hawaiʻi's football team wins their first outright WAC title in twenty-nine years, capturing the hearts of the entire state along the way. The Warriors then beat the University of Washington to complete their undefeated season. The Warriors are selected to play in the Sugar Bowl in New Orleans. They lose to the Georgia Bulldogs.

2008

January 8—A golden era ends as Warriors football coach June Jones leaves for SMU.

February 26—Genoa Keawe, longtime Island entertainer, teacher, and mentor, dies at age eighty-nine.

March 25—The Molokaʻi Ranch decides to quit the island, laying off workers and closing access to its property.

March 31—Aloha Air, after filing for bankruptcy, shuts down after sixty-one years.

July 3—In Rome, Pope Benedict XVI and Jose Cardinal Saraiva Martins promulgate a decree verifying two miracles attributed to Father Damien; this decree is needed before Father Damien can be canonized as a saint.

INDEX

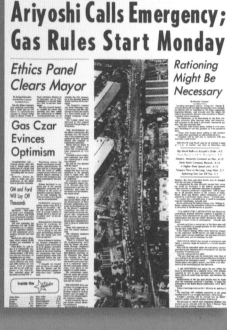